POLICE

USE OF FORCE

A Line Officer's Guide

POLICE

USE OF FORCE

A Line Officer's Guide

Thomas T. Gillespie
Darrel G. Hart
John D. Boren

VARRO PRESS
KANSAS CITY

POLICE
USE OF FORCE
A Line Officer's Guide

Thomas T. Gillespie
Darrel G. Hart
John D. Boren

VARRO PRESS

P.O. Box 8413 – Shawnee Mission, Kansas 66208 USA

Publisher's Cataloging-in-Publication
(Provided by Quality Books, Inc.)

Gillespie, Thomas T., 1947-
    Police use of force: a line officer's guide/Thomas T. Gillespie, Darrel G. Hart, John D. Boren. — 1st ed.
    p. cm
    Includes index.
    Preassigned LCCN: 98-60230
    ISBN: 1-888644-82-6

    1. Police discretion—United States—Handbooks, manuals, etc. 2. Arrest—United States. I. Hart, Darrel G., 1958- II. Boren,m John D., 1940- III.Title.

HV7936.D54G55 1998   363.2'32
                                           QB198-838

Printed and bound in the United States of America

Contents

Foreword

by

Stephen M. Bunting
Captain, University of Delaware Police
Executive Director, American Society of
Law Enforcement Trainers
Use-of-Force Trainer and Expert

Police everywhere have been placed under the proverbial microscope when it comes to the use of force. The proliferation of video cameras in the hands of citizens has resulted in the capturing of many use-of-force incidents on tape. Simultaneously, the same technology has facilitated the widespread installation of video cameras in patrol cars. For the most part, this technology has been beneficial to law enforcement with video documentation justifying the actions of officers.

However, few of us can forget the Rodney King incident. Opinions will differ greatly over the appropriateness of the force used by the officers, and it is certainly not the intent here to judge the actions of those officers. What is indisputable, however is that the Rodney King incident did more to bring public focus to bear upon the use of force by police than any other incident in recent memory.

Putting aside all the negative outcomes of the King incident, the incident did result in many positive changes for law enforcement. Use-of-force training programs were reviewed and revised. In some cases, they were radically overhauled. More time was allocated to use-of-force training through increased training budgets. Finally, use-of-force models in use by many agencies were closely scrutinized.

During the examination of these use-of-force models, most were found to be lacking. Many agencies lacked any model to use for either training or post-incident analysis. Some of the models examined were created by experts for use in court and were very open ended to enable the opinions of the expert to vary depending on the case at hand. Simply put, they were not intended to be used to train officers. Some of the models in place dealt only with the actions of the aggressor but did not give the officer's corresponding appropriate responses. In short, law enforcement was in need of good use-of-force models both to train their officers and to use for post-incident analysis. The models needed to be simple enough to apply during high stress encounters and yet complex enough to be all encompassing.

Out of this need the Reactive Control Model evolved. While its early development certainly predates the King incident, its arrival upon the law enforcement scene in the aftermath of the King incident is no coincidence and is most fortuitous for law enforcement. The Reactive Control Model was developed by Tom Gillespie, Darrel Hart and John Boren. Their combined law enforcement experience approaches a century in time, crosses the country geographically and covers the gamut of agency types and sizes. Once its development was completed, it was nearly immediately adopted statewide as the use-of-force model for the State of New Mexico. Its acceptance and adoption has rapidly spread since.

I had the good fortune to attend the first Reactive Control Model Use-of-Force Instructor Program in Santa Fe. Having used the model to both train officers and to defend their actions in court, I can easily attest to its effectiveness. Officers, juries and judges alike seem to enjoy its simplicity and find it easy to understand. It removes the ambiguity and makes clear what actions are justifiable and under what circumstances.

Use-of-force encounters are an unfortunate but a very necessary part of law enforcement. With the increasing public awareness and scrutiny that is being brought to bear on this law enforcement function, no officer or administrator can afford to be negligent in this highly litigious area. I strongly encourage you to use this book both as a text for teaching use-of-force concepts and as a reference guide for those involved in post-incident analysis.

We will probably never see the day when force will not have to be used by law enforcement officers. With equal certainty, we will probably never see the day when our legal system isn't clogged with cases alleging excessive use of force by officers. We can, however, reduce the likelihood of losing these cases by improving the way in which we teach and administer the use-of-force function in law enforcement. The Reactive Control Model will assist law enforcement in meeting this challenge. As always, be safe and train to survive.

Preface

The use-of-force model presented in this textbook is the culmination of nearly 8 years of collaboration, experimentation and development. In a broader sense, it is the result of over 60 years of practical law enforcement experience. The authors' combined law enforcement backgrounds, ranging from street patrol duties in cities such as Detroit and Oklahoma City to designing and providing training throughout the United States and abroad, made each of us aware of the need for a simple yet comprehensive use-of-force model. The ideal model must be more than easy to understand; it must also facilitate training that can move from the "bookshelf" to the "street," the place where use-of-force decisions are made. We believe the Reactive Control Model meets both criteria.

The Reactive Control Model (RCM) is the centerpiece of a powerful use-of-force program. The power of this program lies in the fact that is was developed to *train* police officers to make appropriate and reasonable use-of-force decisions, not just to *evaluate* an officer's actions after the fact. The comments we have heard most frequently when training line officers is that investigators assigned to review an incident either have no background in use-of-force training or rely on their own professional experience to determine whether reasonable and proper force was used. Too often this results in "reasonable and proper" not being defined until after an officer has used some level of force.

What is considered appropriate and reasonable force should not be a mysterious or misunderstood concept. A department's use-of-force policy should be clear and understandable to all personnel, from the police chief or sheriff to the line officers and internal affairs investigators. Once the policy is established, the department must then provide a training program that is consistent with that policy. This approach is straightforward and re-

The Reactive Control Model

SUBJECT BEHAVIOR	COOPERATIVE	NON-COOPERATIVE	UNARMED ASSAILANT	ARMED ASSAILANT
SUBJECT'S BEHAVIORAL CUES	Submits to Directions and Custody: • COMPLIANT • RESPONSIVE • FOLLOWS DIRECTIONS	Resists Custody By: • Not Responsive to Directions • Evasive to Questions • Verbal Resistance or Body Posture • Pulling/Moving or Running Away	Resists Custody By: UNARMED THREATENING — UNARMED ATTACK Closes Distance	Resists Custody By: ARMED THREATENING — ARMED ATTACK (Deadly Assault) Closes Distance
CRIMINAL ACTIVITY CUES	Unknown Threat	Type of Criminal Activity Investigating		High Risk Activity
OFFICER MENTAL CONDITION	ALERT	CONTROL	ACTIVE	SURVIVAL
OFFICER'S ACTIONS	Verbal Directions • AUTHORITY • ASSESSMENT • CUSTODY DECISION • POSITIONING • PROCEDURES	Verbal Persuasion EMPTY HAND TECHNIQUES ASSESSMENT • Custody Decision • Close Distance CONTROL BY • Escort Position • Distraction Techniques • Compliance Holds • Leverage Takedowns • Impact Takedowns • Chemical Agents	Verbal Commands SHOW FORCE Draw Baton or Other Intermediate Weapon Assess: • Cover • Distance • Assistance • Retreat	USE FORCE Use Baton or Other Intermediate Weapon • Chemicals • Canine
			Verbal Warnings	Survival Action
			SHOW FORCE Draw Firearm Assess: • Cover • Distance • Assistance • Retreat • Canine	USE FORCE Fire Weapon to Stop Attack

(OFFICER'S ACTIONS marked vertically: P R E S E N C E)

SUBMITS TO CUSTODY ← FORCED CUSTODY & CONTROL PROCEDURES →

xii

moves the ambiguity that has existed in peace officers' minds and in departmental policies for years.

When developing the Reactive Control Model, we made every effort to "keep it simple," which every trainer knows is the most important yet most difficult challenge. And we have had the opportunity to "field test" the program in large, medium and small police and sheriff's agencies. We know it works.

One reason why the RCM works so well is the number of unique features that it presents. These features include:

- Specific types of verbal skills required throughout a subject/officer contact
- Specific subject "behavioral cues" to guide officer response.
- A "criminal activity cues" component that guides mental conditioning, whether you are responding to a call or dealing with suspicious circumstances
- "Show force" and "use force" components
- The dynamics of "closing distance," showing how a subject moves from threatening to attacking
- Levels of officer response that are always one level above subject actions
- Numerous post-incident applications, such as being an outline for report writing and a tool for courtroom testimony

All of these features will have more meaning for you as you study the text. You will come to understand that the Reactive Control Model is actually designed to reduce the number of incidents where force is required. And for those incidents where force must be used, you will see that the model is set up to guide you to use-of-force decisions that are reasonable, proper and effective.

We strongly encourage you to carry the model with you. Refer back to it frequently. It will help you make the toughest decisions you will ever have to make. And it will help you make those decisions in a manner that upholds the highest traditions of our profession.

⋙ **1** ⋘

Introduction to the
Reactive Control Model

Objectives

After completing this chapter, you will be able to

- *Identify the significance of each component of the
  Reactive Control Model's name*
- *Explain the reason why custody procedures are not
  considered a level of force*

Being a peace officer, you have taken an oath to protect and serve your community. As such, you may encounter a situation during your career when you have to use force against one citizen to protect another citizen or yourself. The actions that you take in those few moments will be reviewed and scrutinized many times by different individuals with differing perspectives. Making the right decisions on whether and what level of force should be used are challenging tasks, ones that must be accomplished in a professional, reasonable manner. The Reactive Control Model helps you do that.

Overview of the Reactive Control Model

To get a basic understanding of the Reactive Control Model, consider each component of its name. "Reactive" implies something else is controlling your response. This is important because reasonable force depends on the type of behavior, resistance or

1

actions demonstrated by the individual you are encountering. As the Supreme Court said in the case of *Tennessee v. Garner*, which is discussed in Chapter 11 (see page 89), you have to look at the threat posed by a subject, not just the crime he may have committed. At the same time, the model also shows how to use that criminal action to anticipate the threat you may be facing. This puts you in a better position to react with appropriate force.

The second part of the title is "Control." When you are confronted with a subject who is a threat to the community, your goal is to place that person under control. Using the proper amount of force is often the key to getting someone to comply with your lawful orders. Selecting a level of force below the level of resistance exhibited by the subject can place your life and the lives of other in danger. Just as serious, using more force than is reasonable is a violation of the subject's legal rights and could subject you to criminal and civil sanctions. The model will assist you in determining the level of force that is both reasonable and appropriate for establishing control.

The last component of the title is "Model." By definition, a model is an example or standard of excellence that should be the basis of performance. In law enforcement, any use-of-force model should set standards for training and field performance that are acceptable to the community, the agency and the courts. By being based on what the courts have said about reasonable force and by incorporating steps designed to get a subject to comply without you having to resort to using force, the Reactive Control Model does set those standards.

In order to make the model easy to understand, it is broken into two primary areas: subject behavior and officer reaction. Each of these areas are further broken down as follows:

① **Subject Behavior**	② **Officer Reaction**
Cooperative	Alert
Non-Cooperative	Control
Unarmed Assailant	Active
Armed Assailant	Survival

2 PRIMARY AREAS OF RCM

THE SUBJECT'S ACTIONS DICTATE
THE OFFICER'S ACTIONS !

SUBJECT BEHAVIOR	COOPERATIVE	NON-COOPERATIVE	UNARMED ASSAILANT	ARMED ASSAILANT
SUBJECT'S BEHAVIORAL CUES	Submits to Directions and Custody: • COMPLIANT • RESPONSIVE • FOLLOWS DIRECTIONS	Resists Custody By: • Not Responsive to Directions • Evasive to Questions • Verbal Resistance or Body Posture • Pulling/Moving or Running Away	Resists Custody By: UNARMED THREATENING | UNARMED ATTACK — Closes Distance	Resists Custody By: ARMED THREATENING | ARMED ATTACK (Deadly Assault) — Closes Distance
CRIMINAL ACTIVITY CUES	Unknown Threat	Type of Criminal Activity Investigating		High Risk Activity
OFFICER MENTAL CONDITION	ALERT	CONTROL	ACTIVE	SURVIVAL
OFFICER'S ACTIONS P R E S E N C E	Verbal Directions	Verbal Persuasion	Verbal Commands	Verbal Warnings | Survival Action
	• AUTHORITY • ASSESSMENT • CUSTODY DECISION • POSITIONING • PROCEDURES	EMPTY HAND TECHNIQUES ASSESSMENT • Custody Decision • Close Distance CONTROL BY • Escort Position • Distraction Techniques • Compliance Holds • Leverage Takedowns • Impact Takedowns • Chemical Agents	SHOW FORCE Draw Baton or Other Intermediate Weapon | USE FORCE Use Baton or Other Intermediate Weapon Assess: • Cover • Distance • Assistance • Retreat | • Chemicals • Canine	SHOW FORCE Draw Firearm | USE FORCE Fire Weapon to Stop Attack Assess: • Cover • Distance • Assistance • Retreat | • Canine

SUBMITS TO CUSTODY ⟶ FORCED CUSTODY ⟶ FORCED CUSTODY & CONTROL PROCEDURES

This book is divided into four parts: Introduction, Subject Behavior, Officer Reaction, and Legal Issues. In Part Two, Subject Behavior, we present the four general types of behavior that a subject may demonstrate. Then we cover how the subject's criminal activity will impact your response. Last, we show how to mentally prepare yourself to effectively respond to the subject's actions.

Part Three is devoted to proper officer reation in response to the four types of subject behavior. Part Four deals with the legal issues related to police use of force.

What the Model Does Not Cover

NOT CUSTODY PROCEDURES

Before getting into what the Reactive Control Model does cover, you should know what it does not address. The model does not cover custody procedures in detail. These procedures typically include handcuffing, searching, transporting and booking. The reason they are not addressed is that they are generally required for every subject being placed under arrest. As such, they should not be considered uses or levels of force. If they were, they would not be applied universally. If handcuffing was a level of force, you would not handcuff a cooperative person because using force on a compliant subject would be considered unreasonable or excessive.

Force is used to bring an individual under control so you can take him into custody. The custody procedures, especially handcuffing, are designed to maintain that control. If a person resists a physical search or handcuffing, he is not in a cooperative state. You would need to get him back under control, using the level of force dictated by his resistant behavior. The proper response to a resistant subject can be located in the model.

In one sense, handcuffing should be considered a safety procedure in that it protects the subject, the public and you. When arrested, many subjects resist. This might be because they are under the influence of alcohol or drugs, or because they have become psychologically distraught. Securing subjects with handcuffs and placing them in your emergency vehicle protects them

4

from injury and keeps them from attempting to injure you.

However, if the restraint procedures of handcuffing, searching and transporting are not conducted correctly and reasonably, then there is the potential of causing injury or tissue damage. As such, improperly applied custody procedures might be viewed as excessive force. Being a violation of the subject's rights, the officer could be held directly liable and could be criminally prosecuted.

Your agency will determine the reasonable techniques for taking a subject into custody and train you in their proper application. This will likely include protective measures such as double locking handcuffs to ensure that they do not tighten after being applied, properly searching the subject and securing him safely in the vehicle with a seat belt. Once you have been trained in your agency's custody procedures, you should always follow them.

Questions

1. What is the significance of each component of the Reactive Control Model's name?

2. Why are custody procedures not considered uses of force?

3. Under what circumstances could a custody procedure be viewed as a use of force?

4. What are the custody procedures for your agency? When and how should each one be applied?

> ● ALWAYS SEARCH SOMEONE WHEN YOU TAKE THEM INTO CUSTODY; EVEN IF THEY'VE BEEN SEARCHED ALREADY

PART TWO

Subject Behavior

Subject Behavioral Cues

Objectives

After completing this chapter, you will be able to

- *Explain what cues are*
- *Identify the four categories of subject behavioral cues and the characteristics of each*
- *Understand the concept and dynamics of closing distance*
- *Explain what must be present or what must occur for an assault to be classified as a deadly assault*
- *Identify the three categories of deadly weapons*

When responding to a situation, you may be required to make a use-of-force decision to defend yourself, another officer or a member of the public you are sworn to protect. Any response you take is expected to be reasonable and consistent with your departmental policy, procedures and training. To do this, you should rely on subject behavioral cues.

What Are Cues?   "*ACTION TRIGGERS RESPONSE*"

A cue is a behavior or action taken by one person which triggers a certain trained or conditioned response by another person. When most people think of cues, they think of actors. In a play or movie, an actor will not begin his performance until he receives his cue from another actor or the director.

SUBJECT BEHAVIOR	COOPERATIVE	NON-COOPERATIVE	UNARMED ASSAILANT	ARMED ASSAILANT
SUBJECT'S BEHAVIORAL CUES	Submits to Directions and Custody: • COMPLIANT • RESPONSIVE • FOLLOWS DIRECTIONS	Resists Custody By: • Not Responsive to Directions • Evasive to Questions • Verbal Resistance or Body Posture • Pulling/Moving or Running Away	Resists Custody By: UNARMED THREATENING — UNARMED ATTACK Closes Distance	Resists Custody By: ARMED THREATENING — ARMED ATTACK (Deadly Assault) Closes Distance
CRIMINAL ACTIVITY CUES	Unknown Threat	Type of Criminal Activity Investigating		High Risk Activity
OFFICER MENTAL CONDITION	ALERT	CONTROL	ACTIVE	SURVIVAL
OFFICER'S ACTIONS P R E S E N C E	Verbal Directions • AUTHORITY • ASSESSMENT • CUSTODY DECISION • POSITIONING • PROCEDURES	Verbal Persuasion EMPTY HAND TECHNIQUES ASSESSMENT • Custody Decision • Close Distance CONTROL BY • Escort Position • Distraction Techniques • Compliance Holds • Leverage Takedowns • Impact Takedowns • Chemical Agents	Verbal Commands SHOW FORCE — USE FORCE Draw Baton or Other Intermediate Weapon — Use Baton or Other Intermediate Weapon Assess: • Cover • Distance • Assistance • Retreat • Chemicals / • Canine	Verbal Warnings — Survival Action SHOW FORCE — USE FORCE Draw Firearm — Fire Weapon to Stop Attack Assess: • Cover • Distance • Assistance • Retreat • Canine
	SUBMITS TO CUSTODY	FORCED CUSTODY & CONTROL PROCEDURES		

10

It works in much the same way in law enforcement. The actions of the subject are your cues. The type of force that may be required will be based on them. And since those cues guide your response, you can conclude that it is the subject who determines what level of force is reasonable and appropriate.

The Reactive Control Model defines four general types of subject behavioral cues. They are as follows:

- Cooperative
- Non-Cooperative
- Unarmed Assailant
- Armed Assailant

 *4 TYPES OF SUBJECT BEHAVIORAL CUES IN THE RCM*

Cooperative

To be cooperative, a subject must be willing to submit to your directions and custody. You will encounter cooperative subjects in all types of situations, ranging from low-risk vehicle stops to serious felonies in-progress. In fact, the overwhelming majority of interactions involve subjects who are exhibiting this type of behavior.

A subject demonstrates cooperative behavior by showing an understanding of your commands and a willingness to comply with them. In addition, his physical posture and actions should be consistent with a cooperative nature. These might include nodding his head, making eye contact, giving positive, direct responses to your questions and moving in a relaxed, deliberate manner.

Non-Cooperative

The second type of behavioral cue is non-cooperative. Subjects are non-cooperative when they refuse or fail to follow the lawful orders of a peace officer. As such, non-cooperative subjects typically exhibit one or more of the following types of behaviors:

- **Non-Responsive to Directions**—The subject simply stares directly at you with no expression or turns away from you. Non-responsive acts often include refusing to produce identification and ignoring an order.

- **Evasive to Questions**—This can be shown either verbally or non-verbally. Verbal evasiveness is refusing to answer a question or attempting to change the subject away from the object of your investigation. In a non-verbal sense, a subject can be evasive by acting as if he does not understand the question being asked.

- **Verbal Resistance or Body Posture**—This can be best described as subjects who say they will not comply with your orders or who become verbally abusive. A subject may place his hands on his hips, fold his arms on his chest, or brace, tense or flex body muscles to avoid control. Subjects who grab or hang-on to other persons or objects are included in this category.

- **Pulling/Moving or Running Away**—When subjects exhibit this type of behavior, they have moved from passively resisting to actively resisting your efforts to bring them into custody. A low level of active resistance is pulling or jerking away from your grip. Another is simply walking away. A higher level of active resistance is walking away quickly or running after being ordered to stop.

Keep in mind that a simple failure to follow directions does not necessarily mean that a subject is non-cooperative. It is possible that he did not hear or understand your requests. If the situation allows, you should repeat yourself if the subject does not respond. This will enable you to determine whether his behavior is based on a conscious decision to not cooperate or because of situational distractions.

Also, when you attempt to place a subject in custody by escorting him to your vehicle or by placing handcuffs on him, he may begin to struggle and try to wrestle away from your control. As long as you feel the subject is not trying to harm you during this struggle, he is still only an active resister. However, if you perceive he is trying to harm you, he is no longer an active resister. He has initiated an attack and has become an unarmed assailant, the next category of behavior.

Unarmed Assailant   *THREATENING vs. ATTACK*

The third type of subject behavioral cue is unarmed assailant. This category is divided into two distinct forms: unarmed threatening and unarmed attack. Unarmed threatening is where a subject resists custody by verbally or physically threatening to assault you or another citizen. As the name implies, an unarmed attack is where a subject who does not have a weapon initiates a physical attack. Typically, this involves grabbing, punching, kicking, elbowing, biting or any combination of these.   *"CLOSING DISTANCE"*

What takes the subject across the line between an unarmed threat and an unarmed attack is the act of closing distance to the target. To understand the dynamics of closing distance, you must understand the concepts of reaction time and intensity of the attack. Reaction time is the amount of time required for you to recognize you are under attack and determine the proper response or defensive action to take. The intensity of the attack is the speed in which the subject initiates the attack.   *① REACT TIME   ② INTENSITY OF ATTACK*

As illustrated on the next page, an attack commences when the subject begins to close distance by moving toward the target, which may be you, another officer or a private citizen. The speed or intensity in which the subject initiates the attack will have a significant impact on your reaction time. You must perceive the attack or the subject closing distance, make a decision and take action before the subject reaches the point of zero reaction, the point where it will be physically impossible to repel the attack. If you do not take a performance action by then, the attack may be completed. This is illustrated on the following page.

13

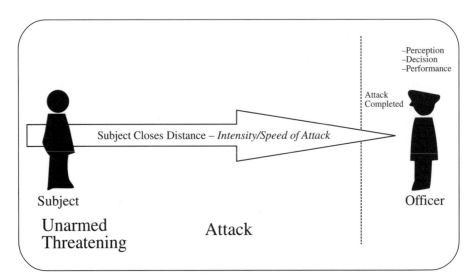

To help grasp this, consider the following breakdown of an unarmed confrontation. An unarmed assailant can threaten you from any distance, usually by making verbal threats and demonstrating the ability to back them up. However, he cannot harm you until he moves close enough to strike you. Since he does not have a weapon, that distance is about one arm's length away or 2 to 3 feet. You must take a defensive action before he reaches that distance or he will be too close for you to repel the attack.

However, at a distance of two arms' length or 6 to 8 feet, you should have time to effectively respond. The subject is in position to complete an attack quickly; he is only one step away from being able to strike you. But if you take a defensive "show force" posture by drawing your baton to the "ready" position before he reaches one arm's length, you will be prepared to defend against a punch, kick or other type of unarmed attack.

The intensity of the attack will have a significant impact on your reaction time. Obviously, if a person is running towards you, you need to react more quickly than if he is slowly shuffling or walking. The speed of the attack and the distance that the attacker must cover directly impact the amount of time you have to make a decision on the proper performance action and then take that action. A high intensity attack greatly reduces that time.

A couple of other points need to be made about an unarmed

attack. First, while foot movement is the most common method of closing distance, other methods include moving closer by swinging punches, grabbing or kicking at you. You must constantly assess an unarmed assailant's distance from you. As the subject closes to about 2 arms' length or 6 to 8 feet away, you must take a performance action using appropriate defensive techniques. These will be discussed in Chapter Seven.

Second, typically an unarmed attacker can cause an injury but usually does not pose a threat of serious bodily harm or loss of life. However, should the subject be significantly larger than you or demonstrate superior fighting skills, or should you be confronted by multiple unarmed subjects, it is possible that you might perceive yourself to be under a deadly assault. In a case such as that, the unarmed subject could be considered to be in the same category as an armed assailant. This is considered a disparity of force, which is discussed in detail in Chapter Four.

"LARGER & MULTIPLE SUBJECTS"

Armed Assailant

As with an unarmed assailant, an armed assailant can either be threatening or attacking. The fact that the subject has a weapon, however, increases the danger of serious or deadly injury to you or another person. The use of a weapon often classifies the attack as a deadly assault. And as just stated, a deadly assault could take place even though a weapon may not be present, depending upon the size, skill and number of assailants.

Simply put, an armed attack or deadly assault occurs whenever there is a fear of serious bodily injury or the potential for loss of life. It is important to understand that the threat initially presented is based on your perception or, as the courts have held, a reasonable belief that a deadly attack was occurring or was about to occur. As long as you have a reasonable belief that an assailant has initiated an attack that could result in serious bodily harm or the loss of your life or the life of another, whatever action you take to stop the attack should be considered justified.

In order for a weapon to be considered deadly, the officer must believe that it is capable of causing serious bodily injury.

There are three types of injuries that fit this definition.

Injuries Classified as Serious Bodily Injuries

3 TYPES OF INJURIES

• **Large, gaping wound**—Can result in the loss of large amounts of blood or shock and can create the potential for serious injury to life-sustaining organs or the nervous system.

• **Major internal organ damage**—Can prevent an organ critical to sustaining life from functioning properly. Among the major organs are the brain, heart, lungs, liver, kidneys and the system of arteries.

• **Major bone breakage**—The fracture or breakage of a major bone could lead to incapacitation and an inability to defend yourself from continued attack. It can also indirectly contribute to the serious damage of organs or the nervous system which can be fatal. Major bones include the forearm, upper arm, thigh, lower leg, ribs, skull and spinal column.

The weapons that can cause serious bodily injuries are also classified into three broad categories, each comprised of several different types. While a few of these weapons can cause only one or two types of life threatening injuries, most can inflict all three.

Weapons Frequently Causing Serious Bodily Injuries

3 TYES OF WEAPONS

• **Firearms**—The most common firearms used against citizens and officers are handguns. Although not very accurate, they are easily concealed and can be deadly when a bullet strikes the human body. Rifles and shotguns are powerful and can be accurately fired from a greater distance than handguns. Certain types of explosive devices can be grouped with firearms, although they are not as commonly used. These include dynamite, concussion grenades and Molotov cocktails.

- **Cutting/stabbing/hacking instruments**—These are any weapons with sharp points or edges that give them the capability to penetrate or cut open the body. Among them are knives, axes, hatchets, machetes, arrows and glass (frequently from broken bottles or windows). Any edged weapon can cause a life-threatening injury, no matter how large it is. Even a very small edged weapon can be extremely dangerous when in the hands of an angry, drunk or drugged subject.

- **Blunt trauma instruments**—A wide variety of weapons can be classified as blunt trauma instruments. Some examples are bats, pipes, bricks, boards, ax handles, cue sticks, tire tools and motorized vehicles. If an assailant has specialized training or is much larger physically, it is possible that his fists and feet could be classified as blunt trauma weapons. The same could be true if you are faced with multiple subjects.

Just as with an unarmed assault, the action that takes an armed subject from threatening to attacking is closing distance. A subject is threatening if he is verbally or physically demonstrating the intent to attack. The attack itself begins when the subject initiates movement toward you. As stated earlier, the components of an officer's reaction time are the recognition of an attack and the formulation of a response decision. When that decision is made, the officer must then execute the defensive action to stop the attack before the subject is able to close the distance to the point of zero reaction. This is illustrated on the following page. *IMPACTS ON REACTION TIME*

In an armed confrontation, there are several factors that can have a significant impact on reaction time. First, in many situations, officers fail to recognize the danger. Armed attacks have often taken place so quickly that the officers involved did not recognize they were under attack. And when they finally did re-

17

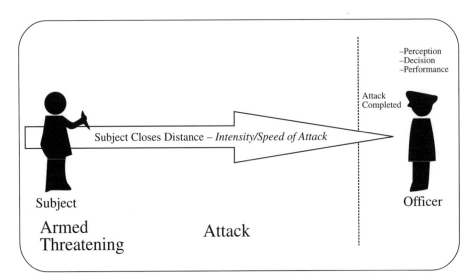

-Perception
-Decision
-Performance

Attack Completed

Subject Closes Distance – *Intensity/Speed of Attack*

Subject

Officer

Armed Threatening

Attack

alize the danger, they were not mentally or physically prepared to take the appropriate defensive action. These may be reasons why some officers have been shot in the line of duty without having unholstered their firearm.

② Another factor impacting reaction time is the number of distractions at the scene. There are any number of possible distractions, with multiple suspects, crowds and noise being among those frequently encountered. Back-up officers can also be a distraction because you have to coordinate your efforts with theirs. The effect of multiple distractions can cause your reaction time to increase significantly. Our studies have shown this increase can be as high as a multiple of three. In other words, you might need 3 times as long to perceive an attack, make a performance decision and execute a defensive action.

③ A third factor affecting reaction time relates to your firearm. In most cases, the appropriate countermeasure to an armed attack is the firing of your weapon to stop the attack. To accomplish this, you must draw your weapon, point it at the subject and pull the trigger. When a weapon is in the holster, the speed in which a properly trained officer can perform these tasks usually ranges from 1.5 to 2.0 seconds. The best time for an expert is about 1.0 second. On the other hand, if the weapon is already out of your holster and at the ready-to-fire position as a show of force, the average speed for firing the weapon is about 0.5 seconds. That is about twice as fast as the best time recorded by expert marksman with a holstered handgun. Even with multiple distractions, you would still be able to fire the weapon within about 1.5 seconds.

The reaction time available will be based on the type of weapon being used by the subject. For a firearm, the amount of reaction time is often very short. A subject who has a weapon in its effective firing range begins to close distance when he moves the weapon towards you. Once the firearm is pointed at you, the attack will be completed as there will be no time for you to react, even if you are pointing your weapon at the subject. Depending on the intensity of the attack, a subject who has a firearm in his hand may be able to initiate and complete an attack in less than 0.5 seconds. This means the acts of closing distance and completing the attack can take place almost simultaneously.

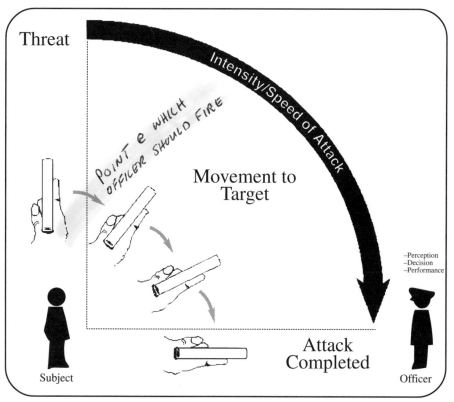

With cutting, stabbing or hacking weapons as well as blunt trauma instruments, the distance of the subject from you is an important factor. Our research has shown that an assailant with a knife can cover 21 to 30 feet and strike an officer in about 1.5 seconds. The 1.5 second mark is critical because, even with multiple distractions, you should still have time to verbally warn the subject to stop and effectively discharge your firearm to counter the attack should he continue to close distance. This is assuming, of course, that your weapon is in the "ready" or show force position. This is discussed further in Chapter Eight.

Once again, the intensity of the attack and the distance that the subject must cover to carry out the attack are the key components of officer reaction time. You must ensure that you take a defensive action to stop the attack before the subject reaches a position in which the attack cannot be repelled, the point of zero reaction. It is very difficult to provide exact distances in which an officer should take a performance action. This is due to the variations in the speed of each attack, the type of weapon being used by the subject and the information that the officer is processing at the scene. Through training, you should be able to develop the knowledge and skills necessary to react and counter an attack by various types of unarmed and armed assailants.

Questions

1. What is a cue?

2. What are the four types of subject behavioral cues? What are the characteristics of each?

3. What are the two types of confrontations that can occur when encountering an unarmed or armed assailant? Explain what each one is.

4. Identify and explain what act takes an assailant over the line from a threat to an attack?

5. When it comes to an attack, what is meant by officer reaction time? What is the point of zero reaction?

6. What are the two types of confrontations that can occur when encountering an armed assailant? Explain what each one is and what takes an assailant over the line from one to the other.

7. Define serious bodily injury and list the types of injuries that are associated with it.

8. What types of weapons can cause serious bodily harm?

9. What factors can impact reaction time in a deadly attack?

⋙ **3** ⋘

Criminal Activity Cues

"TYPE OF CALL"

Objectives

After completing this chapter, you will be able to

- *Identify the limitations of subject behavioral cues*
- *Explain what criminal activity cues are*
- *Explain what is meant by the extension of violence*
- *List the types of criminal activity cues*

As shown in the previous chapter, subject behavioral cues are the primary determinants of what force should be used. However, they alone do not provide all of the information you need to properly respond to many incidents. The Reactive Control Model takes this into account and offers additional guides to assist you.

The Limitations of Subject Behavioral Cues

There are a couple of reasons why you cannot rely solely on subject behavioral cues. First, if you only use behavioral cues, you cannot begin to evaluate a situation until after coming in contact with a subject. Should the incident involve weapons or a fight, you may not have time to shift to the proper mental condition and respond effectively using high-risk tactics. For instance, if you are answering an armed robbery call but do not mentally shift to a survival mode until the subject threatens you with a weapon, you may not be able to react fast enough to defend yourself or another person.

A second limitation is that behavioral cues can be deceptive. While a subject appears to be cooperative, an unknown threat level may exist. Consider the example of a domestic disturbance. High emotions and stress are usually present, but they may not be outwardly apparent; they may be just below the surface. So while the subjects seem friendly and responsive, the situation could easily escalate into an extremely dangerous incident. You can prepare yourself mentally to deal with the potential escalation by using criminal activity cues.

What Are Criminal Activity Cues?

ANTICIPATED BEHAVIORS

While subject cues are behaviors you observe, criminal activity cues point to behaviors you should anticipate encountering, both while responding to an incident and while conducting your investigation. More often than not, you will encounter certain types of subject behavior when responding to certain calls for service. This allows you to prepare for an encounter even though you may not have yet made contact with a subject. For example, all officers know that domestic disturbances are potentially very dangerous. So when you receive a call to respond to a domestic disturbance, you can prepare mentally for such an encounter by reviewing your experience and training on these types of calls. By the same token, if you were to respond to a silent bank alarm with the expectation that it is probably a false alarm, you may not be mentally prepared to deal with an armed suspect if one should flee the bank as you pull up. The purpose of criminal activity cues is to ensure that you are mentally, physically and tactically prepared to react appropriately to a subject's actions, even if you have not yet arrived on the scene.

Assessing the level of threat is crucial. Many deaths and injuries to law enforcement officers are the result of what is known as the extension of violence. This is where a subject who is engaged in violent criminal behavior prior to your arrival focuses the threat on you as soon as you get there. For instance, an armed robbery suspect may have a gun pointed at his victim. When a

24

law enforcement officer arrives at the scene, the weapon will likely be turned on the officer.

If you knew you were responding to an armed robbery in-progress, you could anticipate the potential for an armed confrontation. With this information, you would be in a better position to handle the call effectively. Too often officers arrive at scenes mentally unprepared to deal with the action taking place. This may be one reason why incidents have occurred where officers have been shot in the line of duty while their weapons were still in their holsters.

The three classifications of criminal activity cues are listed below. A chart showing them is on the next page.

Types of Criminal Activity Cues   *3 TYPES*

- **Unknown Threat**—There is not enough intelligence about an incident for you to draw any conclusions about the subject's behavior. It might also be a threat you could not know about in advance. Many subjects who have just committed a crime appear very cooperative when stopped by an officer. This does not mean they are not dangerous; it could be that they are waiting for an opportunity to overpower or injure you.

- **Type of Criminal Activity Investigating**—As stated earlier, certain criminal activities lead to certain predictable behaviors. When you are assigned to investigate a "suspicious person," you should try to find out what sort of activity the subject is engaged in. Based on your experience and training, you can use this information to predict the level of threat you are likely to face. Other factors to consider include location of the call, time of day and what you notice as you arrive at the scene. Also, as you are investigating a crime, you should ensure that your mental condition is consistent with the type of criminal activity.

SUBJECT BEHAVIOR	COOPERATIVE	NON-COOPERATIVE	UNARMED ASSAILANT	ARMED ASSAILANT
SUBJECT'S BEHAVIORAL CUES	Submits to Directions and Custody: • COMPLIANT • RESPONSIVE • FOLLOWS DIRECTIONS	Resists Custody By: • Not Responsive to Directions • Evasive to Questions • Verbal Resistance or Body Posture • Pulling/Moving or Running Away	Resists Custody By: UNARMED THREATENING / UNARMED ATTACK Closes Distance	Resists Custody By: ARMED THREATENING / ARMED ATTACK (Deadly Assault) Closes Distance

CRIMINAL ACTIVITY CUES	Unknown Threat	Type of Criminal Activity Investigating		High Risk Activity

OFFICER MENTAL CONDITION	ALERT	CONTROL	ACTIVE	SURVIVAL
OFFICER'S ACTIONS	Verbal Directions • AUTHORITY • ASSESSMENT • CUSTODY DECISION • POSITIONING • PROCEDURES	Verbal Persuasion EMPTY HAND TECHNIQUES ASSESSMENT • Custody Decision • Close Distance CONTROL BY • Escort Position • Distraction Techniques • Compliance Holds • Leverage Takedowns • Impact Takedowns	Verbal Commands SHOW FORCE Draw Baton or Other Intermediate Weapon ASSESS: • Cover • Distance • Assistance • Retreat USE FORCE Use Baton or Other Intermediate Weapon • Chemicals • Canine	Verbal Warnings | Survival Action SHOW FORCE Draw Firearm | USE FORCE Fire Weapon to Stop Attack Assess: • Cover • Distance • Assistance • Retreat • Canine

P R E S E N C E

SUBMITS TO CUSTODY ←----- Chemical Agents -----←←←← FORCED CUSTODY & CONTROL PROCEDURES →→→→

- **High-Risk Activity**—This includes any activity where there is a potential for violence or the use of a weapon by the subject. Some examples of high-risk calls include a domestic disturbance, silent bank alarm, shots fired, an armed robbery in-progress or a man with a gun.

Criminal activity cues can be determined through a number of sources. These include the dispatch, witnesses, other officers and, most importantly, your own observations. The more information you gather, the more accurate your threat assessment will be.

Each incident will be different, so you cannot always accurately forecast the level of threat. In addition, it is possible for the same criminal activity to result in different types of responses. For example, a burglary could range from an unknown threat to a high-risk activity. If you receive a call to see a person whose home was broken into while he was away over the weekend, you could probably expect a very low level of threat. However, if the caller states that suspects were spotted leaving the scene, the threat would be higher. The risk should be considered higher still if you are responding to a burglary in progress. If there is a doubt about the criminal activity cue or should more than one cue exist, you should base your preparation on the highest level of potential threat.

Questions

1. What are the limitations of relying solely on subject behavioral cues? Why is each one dangerous?

2. What are criminal activity cues? How are they different from subject behavioral cues?

3. What is meant by the extension of violence?

4. List and explain the types of criminal activity cues? What are some examples of each?

5. What are some sources of criminal activity cues?

⪻ 4 ⪼
Establishing the Proper
Mental Condition

Objectives

After completing this chapter, you will be able to

- *Identify the four types of officer mental conditions*
- *Understand the importance of mental condition when it comes to the use of force*
- *Know how to use subject behavioral and criminal activity cues to establish the proper mental condition*
- *Understand the impact of a disparity of force*

The subject behavioral and criminal activity cues outline the types of behaviors you are likely to encounter. While they indicate how to react in a reasonable manner, they can also help you prepare to make those reactions. You should use those cues to set your mental state of readiness.

Officer Mental Conditions

Your mental condition is critical to the success of each response. If you are mentally prepared, you will have a better chance of influencing the subject to make the right decision, which is to comply with your lawful orders. If you are not, you may be positioning yourself to use a level of force that is either less effective or excessive.

The Reactive Control Model uses four basic mental conditions. They are as follows.

Types of Officer Mental Conditions

- **Alert**—You must be alert at all times. Because you wear a uniform and represent authority, your mere presence and the actions you take will influence the people you come into contact with. You must always be prepared for even the most routine situation to change quickly, possibly escalating to a higher level of threat.

- **Control**—When in this mode, you try to establish order and control at a scene. This mental condition requires a more assertive, yet persuasive approach than the alert mode. At the same time, you must be cautious because being assertive creates a heightened risk; many people simply choose not to cooperate with law enforcement officers, no matter what. Although the risk encountered in this mode is generally low, it has the potential to escalate, depending upon the subject's response to your requests or actions.

- **Active**—You enter the active mode whenever you encounter or anticipate encountering an unarmed act of violence or an unarmed assailant. Being active is being prepared to respond in a reasonable manner without hesitation. This requires a more intense, focused mental condition than is necessary when in the control mode.

- **Survival**—If a subject is armed or if criminal activity cues indicate a potential for a deadly confrontation, you must be in the survival mode. This means being mentally prepared to take whatever action is necessary to protect yourself, other officers and the general public.

SUBJECT BEHAVIOR		COOPERATIVE	NON-COOPERATIVE	UNARMED ASSAILANT	ARMED ASSAILANT
SUBJECT'S BEHAVIORAL CUES		Submits to Directions and Custody: • COMPLIANT • RESPONSIVE • FOLLOWS DIRECTIONS	Resists Custody By: • Not Responsive to Directions • Evasive to Questions • Verbal Resistance or Body Posture • Pulling/Moving or Running Away	Resists Custody By: UNARMED THREATENING | UNARMED ATTACK — Closes Distance	Resists Custody By: ARMED THREATENING | ARMED ATTACK (Deadly Assault) — Closes Distance
CRIMINAL ACTIVITY CUES		Unknown Threat	Type of Criminal Activity Investigating		High Risk Activity
OFFICER MENTAL CONDITION		ALERT	CONTROL	ACTIVE	SURVIVAL
OFFICER'S ACTIONS	P R E S E N C E	Verbal Directions • AUTHORITY • ASSESSMENT • CUSTODY DECISION • POSITIONING • PROCEDURES	Verbal Persuasion — EMPTY HAND TECHNIQUES — ASSESSMENT • Custody Decision • Close Distance — CONTROL BY • Escort Position • Distraction Techniques • Compliance Holds • Leverage Takedowns • Impact Takedowns	Verbal Commands — SHOW FORCE Draw Baton or Other Intermediate Weapon — Assess: • Cover • Distance • Assistance • Retreat | USE FORCE Use Baton or Other Intermediate Weapon • Chemicals • Canine	Verbal Warnings | Survival Action — SHOW FORCE Draw Firearm — Assess: • Cover • Distance • Assistance • Retreat | USE FORCE Fire Weapon to Stop Attack • Canine

• Chemical Agents

SUBMITS TO CUSTODY ← → FORCED CUSTODY & CONTROL PROCEDURES → SUBMITS TO CUSTODY

Using Cues to Establish Mental Condition

You establish the proper mental condition by reacting to the available cues. **Before making contact with a subject, you should rely on the criminal activity cues.** These will enable you to match your level of preparedness with the type of behavior you anticipate finding once you arrive on scene. Over time, you will develop a sense about which subject behaviors are associated with various types of criminal activity.

At the point of making contact and while investigating an incident, you should use both the criminal activity and subject behavioral cues. It is possible that they may not be consistent. For example, consider a case where a stop is made of a vehicle matching the description of one involved in an armed robbery. While the criminal activity cue dictates using survival tactics, the subject's behavior may be totally cooperative, indicating only an alert response.

You may find the opposite situation to exist, as well. You may be sent to take a report on a stolen bicycle, a relatively low threat call. Upon arriving at the scene, you see two men on the sidewalk, one holding a bike, the other standing with a child. As you approach, the two men begin fighting. In this case, the category of the criminal activity cue was initially "Alert," but the subject behavioral cues you observed upon arriving at the scene were "Active."

If the subject behavior cues and criminal activity cues do not match, your mental preparation should be based on the highest level of threat. In the first example, you should tactically operate in the survival mode. If your investigation determines the subject is not the armed robber, then your mental condition should shift down to the alert mode. In the second example, what seemed to be a routine report call has turned into a higher level confrontation. You begin by being mentally alert and shift tactically to the active mode until you are able to separate the combatants and restore order.

Always keep in mind that any situation can rapidly escalate or de-escalate. You have to be mentally prepared to escalate and de-escalate just as quickly, depending on the situation and subject's actions.

Disparity of Force

There is another area that should be discussed here since it will have a significant impact on your mental preparation and condition throughout an incident. It is known as the disparity of force. The disparity of force is the unequal advantage of one person or a group of individuals over another person due to size, strength, special skills, training or number of combatants. From a law enforcement officer's perspective, it can be either positive or negative.

A positive disparity of force occurs when an officer or officers have a clear advantage over a subject or subjects. As mentioned earlier, your presence alone may lead to a positive disparity of force. As a law enforcement officer, you wear a distinctive uniform, display a badge, carry a handgun in a holster and drive a vehicle that is clearly marked. The purpose of these visual symbols are to ensure that the public is immediately aware of an officer's authority and responsibility. The symbols that allow you to be readily identifiable also provide you with a psychological and physical advantage over the individuals who choose to follow the established rules and laws of society. Fortunately for us, that's most of the people we come in contact with.

Another form of positive disparity of force is where officers outnumber the subjects on-scene. This type of situation will enable the officers to employ a tactic known as "contact and cover," where only one officer maintains verbal contact with the subject while the other officers provide back-up cover. This tactic is discussed further in later chapters.

While a positive disparity of force works to your advantage, a negative disparity of force can work against you. For example, you may respond to a call for a disturbance-in-progress where the person causing the disturbance is 6' 5" tall, very muscular and weighs about 250 pounds. If you are significantly smaller in terms of height, weight and build, you would likely conclude that the subject may have an advantage over you. You might also draw the same conclusion if the subject is demonstrating superior skills in the area of martial arts or if you are outnumbered by multiple subjects, regardless of what their physical characteristics or skills are. A negative disparity would tilt any use-of-force confrontation in favor of the subject if both the subject and officer used equal levels of force.

You have the right and the duty to defend yourself from attack. The Reactive Control Model advocates and was designed to ensure that an officer always maintains a positional and tactical advantage over individuals, even if they do have the advantage of size, strength, training, location of incident or numbers of persons. Thus, to counteract a perceived negative disparity of force, you could view the subject as posing a higher level of threat. This would enable you to select a level of response necessary to successfully control the subject while protecting your safety and the safety of others.

In determining what level of threat could be reasonably assigned, thereby establishing an appropriate level of force that could be used, you must rely on good judgment. What is meant by good judgment in an incident such as this? For the most part, it is properly assessing and employing the options that are available to you, which will likely include requesting back-up officers to assist, using cover or concealment, disengaging (retreating) and using clear, strong verbal communications skills. While this book discusses these options and the decision-making process on using them, good judgment in making those decisions is developed through sound training and experience.

One last point needs to be made. A disparity of force can emerge at any time during an incident and can shift back and forth between positive and negative. So while you may perceive to have a positive disparity of force when contact is first made, it can switch to negative depending upon how the incident unfolds. The reverse can also be true; a negative disparity of force can quickly shift to positive.

Given that each encounter will be different and dynamic, you must be prepared at all times to react as the situation dictates. Your response to an incident will be evaluated based on the facts of the incident as well as the standard of reasonableness. The rest of the chapters in this book will help you make the response decisions that can stand scrutiny.

Questions

1. Why is being in the proper mental condition essential to the success of each response?

2. What are the four officer mental conditions? How are they different from each other?

3. How do you establish the proper mental condition before arriving at a scene? How do you establish it after making contact?

4. What should you do if there is a conflict between the mental conditions dictated by criminal activity cues and subject behavioral cues?

5. What is meant by a disparity of force?

6. How is it that a disparity of force can be considered either positive or negative?

7. How does the Reactive Control Model deal with a disparity of force?

❧ PART THREE ❧

Officer Reaction

⋘ 5 ⋙

Reacting to a
Cooperative Subject

Objectives

After completing this chapter, you will be able to:

- *Adopt the appropriate "cooperative" mental condition*
- *Explain how to give verbal directions*
- *Identify the proper steps for dealing with a cooperative subject*

In the previous section, we discussed the general categories of subject behavior cues, criminal activity cues and how to mentally prepare yourself to deal with them. Now we move on to the proper officer response.

Officer Reaction to Cooperative Cues

Since you are a figure of authority, your presence will have a significant impact on people and situations. Therefore, you must always be alert when interacting with the public. Fortunately, the vast majority of your responses will be with subjects who are compliant, responsive and willing to follow directions.

When you encounter a cooperative subject, you should give clear verbal directions so he knows what is expected of him. Poor communication skills could cause a seemingly harmless situation to escalate into a serious incident. Some steps for giving clear verbal directions are listed on page 41.

Use of Force Continuum

SUBJECT BEHAVIOR	COOPERATIVE	NON-COOPERATIVE	UNARMED ASSAILANT	ARMED ASSAILANT
SUBJECT'S BEHAVIORAL CUES	Submits to Directions and Custody: • COMPLIANT • RESPONSIVE • FOLLOWS DIRECTIONS	Resists Custody By: • Not Responsive to Directions • Evasive to Questions • Verbal Resistance or Body Posture • Pulling/Moving or Running Away	Resists Custody By: UNARMED THREATENING UNARMED ATTACK Closes Distance	Resists Custody By: ARMED THREATENING ARMED ATTACK (Deadly Assault) Closes Distance

CRIMINAL ACTIVITY CUES	Unknown Threat	Type of Criminal Activity Investigating		High Risk Activity

OFFICER MENTAL CONDITION	ALERT	CONTROL	ACTIVE	SURVIVAL
OFFICER'S ACTIONS	Verbal Directions • AUTHORITY • ASSESSMENT • CUSTODY DECISION • POSITIONING • PROCEDURES	Verbal Persuasion EMPTY HAND TECHNIQUES ASSESSMENT • Custody Decision • Close Distance CONTROL BY • Escort Position • Distraction Techniques • Compliance Holds • Leverage Takedowns • Impact Takedowns • Chemical Agents	Verbal Commands SHOW FORCE Draw Baton or Other Intermediate Weapon Assess: • Cover • Distance • Assistance • Retreat	USE FORCE Use Baton or Other Intermediate Weapon • Chemicals • Canine	Verbal Warnings SHOW FORCE Draw Firearm Assess: • Cover • Distance • Assistance • Retreat • Canine	Survival Action USE FORCE Fire Weapon to Stop Attack

P R E S E N E C E — SUBMITS TO CUSTODY .... FORCED CUSTODY & CONTROL PROCEDURES

40

Steps for Giving Verbal Directions

- **Be clear and concise.** There should be no doubt in the subject's mind about why you have contacted him and specifically what you want him to do.

- **Use your normal voice.** As long as a person is being cooperative, there is no need to lower or raise your voice. Speak in a normal tone.

- **Be courteous, yet firm.** Treat all persons with respect and courtesy. Cooperative people may become belligerent if they feel they are being mistreated or that you are too authoritative. At the same time, be firm so that a subject gets the impression that you expect your directions to be followed.

Even if you use effective verbal communication skills, a situation can escalate, often very rapidly and for no apparent reason. Given this, there are other steps you should take when dealing with a cooperative subject.

Steps for Dealing with a Cooperative Subject

- **Authority**—Quickly establish yourself as the person in control of the situation. Since your uniform projects an image of authority, your arrival at the scene should have a positive impact in establishing your authority. If you are in plainclothes, identify yourself as a peace officer to ensure that there is no confusion as to your lawful authority.

- **Assessment**—Gather as much information as you can about the situation. Evaluate the subject's actions and responses to your questions. Conduct a personal observation of the scene. Also, interview all witnesses and other reliable sources.

- **Custody Decision**—After compiling all possible data, make a fair and objective decision on whether to release the subject or take him into custody. You must remember that a subject can be legally taken into custody only after you have established probable cause that he has committed, is committing or is about to commit a crime.

- **Positioning**—Before approaching a cooperative subject to take him into custody, instruct him to adopt a position that is safe for both him and you. You should be guided by your training, agency policy and procedures in this area.

- **Procedures**—Follow the procedures set by your agency for performing the arrest function. Typically, these include handcuffing, searching, transporting and booking.

Throughout the encounter, you should be alert for changes in the subject's behavior. Unless he ceases to be cooperative, however, you must not move up to a higher level of response. Should a subject shift from cooperative to another behavioral level, his new behavior will dictate the amount of force necessary to maintain or regain control. As long as you continue to react to the subject's actions in a reasonable manner, your response should be judged to be appropriate.

Questions

1. What mental condition should you be in when dealing with a cooperative subject?

2. What are the proper steps for giving verbal directions?

3. What are the proper steps for dealing with a cooperative subject?

⋘ 6 ⋙

Reacting to a
Non-Cooperative Subject

Objectives

After completing this chapter, you will be able to

- *Adopt the appropriate "non-cooperative" mental condition*
- *List the proper steps for confronting a non-cooperative subject*

$\mathbf{A}$ subject can be described as being non-cooperative if he is not compliant or non-responsive to your directions. When confronted with a subject who is passively or actively resisting, your mental condition should be in the control mode.

Officer Reaction to Non-Cooperative Cues

Subjects are non-cooperative when they refuse or fail to follow the lawful orders of a peace officer. As discussed in the chapter on subject behavioral cues, a non-cooperative subject typically exhibits one or more of the following types of behavior:

Types of Non-Cooperative Behavior

- **Non-Responsive to Directions**—Examples would be a subject who will not comply with your instructions by staring directly at you with no expression or by

SUBJECT BEHAVIOR	COOPERATIVE	NON-COOPERATIVE	UNARMED ASSAILANT	ARMED ASSAILANT
SUBJECT'S BEHAVIORAL CUES	Submits to Directions and Custody: • COMPLIANT • RESPONSIVE • FOLLOWS DIRECTIONS	Resists Custody By: • Not Responsive to Directions • Evasive to Questions • Verbal Resistance or Body Posture • Pulling/Moving or Running Away	Resists Custody By: UNARMED THREATENING UNARMED ATTACK Closes Distance	Resists Custody By: ARMED THREATENING ARMED ATTACK (Deadly Assault) Closes Distance

CRIMINAL ACTIVITY CUES	Unknown Threat	Type of Criminal Activity Investigating		High Risk Activity

OFFICER MENTAL CONDITION	ALERT	CONTROL	ACTIVE	SURVIVAL
OFFICER'S ACTIONS	Verbal Directions P • AUTHORITY R • ASSESSMENT E • CUSTODY DECISION S • POSITIONING E • PROCEDURES N C E	Verbal Persuasion EMPTY HAND TECHNIQUES ASSESSMENT • Custody Decision • Close Distance CONTROL BY • Escort Position • Distraction Techniques • Compliance Holds • Leverage Takedowns • Impact Takedowns • Chemical Agents →	Verbal Commands SHOW FORCE Draw Baton or Other Intermediate Weapon Assess: • Cover • Distance • Assistance • Retreat	USE FORCE Use Baton or Other Intermediate Weapon • Chemicals • Canine	Verbal Warnings SHOW FORCE Draw Firearm Assess: • Cover • Distance • Assistance • Retreat • Canine	Survival Action USE FORCE Fire Weapon to Stop Attack

SUBMITS TO CUSTODY ←← FORCED CUSTODY & CONTROL PROCEDURES

turning away from you. Non-responsive acts often include refusing to produce identification or following an order when requested.

- **Evasive to Questions**—This behavior can be exhibited by either verbal or non-verbal actions. He may refuse to answer questions or attempt to change the subject away from the focus of your investigation. He may also act as if he did not understand or hear your question.

- **Verbal Resistance or Body Posture**—This behavior is best described as persons who verbally refuse to comply with your requests or become verbally abusive. They may also place their hands on their hips, folds their arms on their chest or brace, tense or flex their muscles to avoid control.

- **Pulling/Moving or Running Away**—When subjects exhibit this type of behavior, they have moved from passively resisting to actively resisting your efforts to bring them into custody. Active resistance can be characterized by the subject attempting to pull, jerk or wrestle away from your grip. Another is simply walking away. A higher level of active resistance is walking away quickly or running after being ordered to stop.

If you are dealing with a non-cooperative subject, you should try to verbally persuade him to cooperate. Many people respond to verbal persuasion, and if the situation allows, you should make an effort to reword your request if the first or subsequent attempts fail. For this reason, your communications skills are extremely important in attempting to convince a subject to comply with your request. Depending on the type of situation you are handling, you should explain the purpose of your request and that his refusal could result in more serious action. At the same time, be alert for signs of communications disabilities that may not be readily evident. The actions of individuals with these types of disabilities may be misinterpreted as evasive or non-cooperative.

The chance of success through verbal communication may decrease as the level of resistance increases. If you are unable to persuade a subject to cooperate and you are placing him under arrest and employing custody procedures, it is advisable to continue to give verbal directions so the subject understands what you expect him to do.

Although you may be making every effort to bring about compliance, there will be a point where you will have to decide whether to arrest or release the subject. The amount of time you take trying to persuade the subject to comply with your request will be based on his actions and will vary from person to person.

If you decide to take the subject into custody, you will have to initiate the contact, which means you will be the one who has to close distance. The act of closing distance and touching the subject may increase the potential for the situation to escalate in intensity. You must be mentally and physically prepared to deal with a higher level of resistance even though it may not occur.

Since a non-cooperative subject usually poses a low threat, the tactics for control are empty-hand techniques. Some of these are listed on the following pages. The techniques on the list are not intended to be used in a progressive or stair-step manner. Each may be independently selected and applied for control of a specific type of subject resistance. Before using an empty-hand technique, however, you should receive training on its proper application.

Techniques for Dealing with Non-Cooperative Subjects

- **Escort Position**—This is accomplished by placing one hand on the subject's upper arm and the other hand on the lower arm or wrist area. Many non-cooperative people become compliant and responsive as soon as they are touched.

• **Distraction Techniques**—If you meet resistance such as pulling arms in and tightening muscles when you try to apply the escort position or compliance technique, consider using a technique that may momentarily direct the subject's attention away from your objective. An action such as bumping or pinching could distract him, possibly giving you the opportunity to gain control.

• **Compliance Holds**—These are used to limit a subject's movements by locking joints and delivering an immediate, temporary pain, usually to the wrists, arms or fingers. Some examples are twist locks, finger locks and goose necks. Pressure sensitive control techniques can be used as passive resistance controls or as distraction techniques. It should be noted here that some individuals have a high tolerance for pain and that drugs or alcohol can desensitize a person. Subjects such as these may require an increased level of control.

• **Leverage Takedowns**—Takedowns are techniques used to limit a subject's movement and place him in a position where you can effectively gain control. This is generally accomplished by forcing him to the floor or ground by using combinations of joint locks and leverages, such as a straight-arm takedown.

• **Impact Takedowns**—This would be similar to a tackle made in football. It could be used if you are chasing a fleeing subject.

• **Chemicals**—Chemicals refer to liquid sprays, foams, gases and irritants that cause discomfort and temporary pain on the skin, eyes and mucous membranes. It is important to note that the use of chemicals puts you across the threshold to utilizing intermediate weapons, although they are not impact weapons and normally do not cause tissue damage. However, because chemicals, gases and irritants can have an adverse effect on some people, you must ensure that proper first aid and medical treatment is administered immediately if needed. You should be guided by your department's policies and procedures on the proper use of chemicals.

Once you have a non-cooperative subject under control, you should follow your agency's arrest and custody procedures. This usually includes handcuffing, searching, transporting and booking. As stated before, it is important that you continue to communicate with the subject throughout the process. Explain that you want him to place his hands behind him for cuffing or that you are going to assist him up off the ground. If the subject decides to become cooperative, he might assist you with these maneuvers.

Questions

1. What mental condition should you be in when confronting a non-cooperative subject?

2. What is the first step you should take when dealing with a non-cooperative subject?

3. Why is closing distance on a non-cooperative subject dangerous?

4. List the various empty-hand techniques that can be used on a non-cooperative subject. Under what circumstances would each one be used?

5. Which empty-hand technique is not really an empty-hand technique? What is your agency's policy on its use?

⋘ 7 ⋙

Reacting to an
Unarmed Assailant

Objectives

After completing this chapter, you will be able to

- *Adopt the appropriate "unarmed assailant" mental condition*
- *List the options for confronting a threatening unarmed assailant*
- *Explain the difference between showing force and using force*
- *List the options for confronting an unarmed assailant*

An unarmed assailant is a person who, without the use of a weapon, threatens or attacks you. Whether he is threatening an attack or actually carrying one out, you must take steps to control the subject and protect yourself. Given the progressive nature of these steps, you should be in an active mental condition.

There is a crucial point that you must keep in mind here. Typically, an unarmed subject can cause an injury should the confrontation escalate but usually does not pose a real threat of serious bodily harm or loss of life. However, if due to a negative disparity of force, such as the subject is significantly larger than you or has demonstrated superior fighting skills, or you are outnumbered, you may believe that there is an opportunity for the subject or subjects to seriously injure you.

SUBJECT BEHAVIOR	COOPERATIVE	NON-COOPERATIVE	UNARMED ASSAILANT	ARMED ASSAILANT
SUBJECT'S BEHAVIORAL CUES	Submits to Directions and Custody: • COMPLIANT • RESPONSIVE • FOLLOWS DIRECTIONS	Resists Custody By: • Not Responsive to Directions • Evasive to Questions • Verbal Resistance or Body Posture • Pulling/Moving or Running Away	Resists Custody By: UNARMED THREATENING — UNARMED ATTACK Closes Distance	Resists Custody By: ARMED THREATENING — ARMED ATTACK (Deadly Assault) Closes Distance
CRIMINAL ACTIVITY CUES	Unknown Threat		Type of Criminal Activity Investigating	High Risk Activity

OFFICER MENTAL CONDITION	ALERT	CONTROL	ACTIVE	SURVIVAL
OFFICER'S ACTIONS	Verbal Directions	Verbal Persuasion	Verbal Commands	Verbal Warnings / Survival Action
P R E S E N C E	• AUTHORITY • ASSESSMENT • CUSTODY DECISION • POSITIONING • PROCEDURES	EMPTY HAND TECHNIQUES ASSESSMENT • Custody Decision • Close Distance CONTROL BY • Escort Position • Distraction Techniques • Compliance Holds • Leverage Takedowns • Impact Takedowns • Chemical Agents	SHOW FORCE Draw Baton or Other Intermediate Weapon Assess: • Cover • Distance • Assistance • Retreat USE FORCE Use Baton or Other Intermediate Weapon • Chemicals • Canine	SHOW FORCE Draw Firearm Assess: • Cover • Distance • Assistance • Retreat USE FORCE Fire Weapon to Stop Attack • Canine
	SUBMITS TO CUSTODY	FORCED CUSTODY & CONTROL PROCEDURES		

50

You are allowed to use whatever force is reasonable to protect yourself or another person from serious injury or death. So even though the subject is unarmed, if you believe you are in life-threatening situation, you should not be operating in the active mental condition. You should be in the survival mode, dealing with the subject in the manner prescribed in the next chapter, "Reacting to an Armed Assailant." Until that time, however, all unarmed subjects should be dealt with in the manner outlined below.

Officer Reaction to Unarmed Threat

A subject is in an unarmed threatening mode when he uses his body, hands and/or feet to physically threaten to attack you or another person. When confronted by an unarmed assailant, your objective is to convince the subject to de-escalate and comply with your directions. While you would try to persuade a non-cooperative subject, you should attempt to convey authority and strength to gain control of a threatening one. He should understand the seriousness of the situation and your commitment to resolve the problem without escalation. To accomplish this, you should give verbal commands if the situation allows.

Steps for Giving Verbal Commands

- **Use concise, straight-forward directives**. These orders should be short and very clear, such as "Move away from the vehicle!", "Place you hands behind your head!" and "Do it now!". You can attempt to reason with a unarmed assailant, but he should get the clear impression that no options are negotiable. He has only one choice: Comply with your orders.

- **Keep your voice strong and firm.** Your orders should be delivered with a sense of commitment and urgency. Control is expressed by your taking charge of the situation.

51

- **Be consistent.** Only one officer should give verbal commands if multiple officers are present. A subject who receives directives from several officers can easily become confused. While the primary officer communicates with the subject, the remaining officers should provide back-up cover. This concept is known as "contact and cover;" it should be established in all situations where multiple officers are dealing with a single subject.

Besides giving verbal commands, you should also **show force**. Since the assailant is unarmed, a reasonable show of force can be drawing an intermediate range weapon such as the baton to the "at ready" position. It is critical that the subject can see the weapon and your willingness to use it should he initiate an attack.

You must understand that there is a distinct difference between showing force and using force. Using force is an action taken by a law enforcement officer that has the potential for causing injury. Drawing a baton or some other intermediate weapon will not result in an injury. A weapon can cause harm only when it is actually used.

There may be situations where an officer is unable to show force due to a surprise or unexpected attack. However, if you have the opportunity to show force, there are three reasons why it is recommended that you do so. They are listed below.

Reasons for Showing Force

WHY SHOW FORCE?

- **Gives the subject a chance to de-escalate.** By showing force when threatened, you have clearly demonstrated your commitment to take action should the subject decide to attack. In addition, the fact that you are prepared to act using your intermediate weapon gives you a clear tactical advantage. Hopefully, these actions will positively influence the subject to cooperate and de-escalate his behavior.

• **Provides an additional level at which to operate.** Without the option of showing force, you will have only two alternatives: using force or not using force. This means you cannot demonstrate a tactical advantage over the subject unless he attacks and the only leverage you have to prevent that attack is your verbal commands. By showing force with an intermediate weapon, however, you have an additional opportunity to convince your assailant to make the correct decision. In this regard, showing force helps protect both him and you.

• **Reduces your reaction time.** If an unarmed assailant closes distance and initiates an attack, you have to mentally process this information and then take steps to defend yourself. If your baton or some other intermediate weapon is still on your belt, you may not have enough time to draw and use it effectively after the attack begins. On the other hand, if it is already drawn and in the "at ready" position, you will be in a better position to protect yourself.

While showing force, you should attempt to make accurate assessments of your situation. These will help determine the best course of action to handle the threat and the attack should the incident escalate.

Unarmed Threat Situational Assessments

• **Cover**—You may be able to reduce your exposure to danger by using on-scene objects for protection. These can include vehicles or fixed barriers when outside and walls and pieces of furniture when inside. When tactically deploying on a scene, the use of cover demonstrates to other officers responding that they, too, should select a position of cover. By taking cover and reducing your exposure, you convey to the subject that you are protected and prepared for a confrontation. This may provide an opportunity for the situation to de-escalate as it may give you a chance to negotiate a safe resolution of the incident.

- **Distance**—Should a subject begin to close distance, you may be able to increase the space between him and you by moving away. Even if you cannot prevent the attack, increasing distance gives you more time to prepare to defend yourself. However, you should only attempt to create distance by moving away if it can be done without placing yourself or another person in a more vulnerable position. Safety is always a prime consideration.

- **Assistance**—If time and manpower allow, request a back-up officer to assist you. Knowing the status of your backup will help determine your actions. The presence of other officers may give you more flexibility in handling the subject than if they are en route or just arriving on-scene.

- **Retreat**—Since your personal safety is a primary consideration, retreat or disengagement to move to a more defensible position should be considered if it can be done **safely**. If you are dealing with multiple assailants, you may need to withdraw to await additional personnel. Keep in mind that in order to consider a tactical withdrawal, you will have to redirect your focus from the subject to selecting a more defensible location. That, in itself, can leave you more vulnerable.

Officer Reaction to Unarmed Attack

When you are confronted by an unarmed assailant, the threat will continue until one of two things happens. Either the subject de-escalates and complies with your instructions, or he initiates the attack by closing distance. If attacked, you may have to use force to defend yourself and gain control of the subject. The timing of your reaction is critical. As stated earlier, a subject initiates an attack when he begins to close distance toward you or another person. If an unarmed assailant is allowed to close distance within one arm's length or 2 to 3 feet, he has reached the point of zero reaction, the point where he will be able land a blow no matter what defensive action you take. As such, you need to take action to defend yourself from the attack as the subject moves to a position of about 4 to 6 feet. This defensive action is also dependent on the intensity or speed of the attack. The faster the subject is moving toward you, the less time you will have to make a decision on the proper defensive action to take and then to take that action.

Intermediate Weapons

Any force that you use must be objectively reasonable. Since your assailant is unarmed, the recommended level of response is an intermediate weapon. An intermediate weapon is one that has the potential for causing tissue damage but a low potential of resulting in serious bodily injury when used properly. As such, it falls between empty-hand techniques which are unlikely to cause serious injury and your firearm which has the potential for causing serious injury or death.

The most common intermediate weapon is the baton, either side handle, straight or expandable. A baton's primary advantage is that its length of reach and the impact power it generates give you a tactical advantage over an unarmed attacker. When using a baton, you will be able to strike an assailant before he is close enough to strike you. Of course, it is important that you receive proper training in the use of a baton to ensure that your strikes are directed to those areas of the body which have low potential for serious bodily injury. You should be guided by your department's training and policy when using an intermediate weapon.

When your primary intermediate weapon is not available, there are some weaponless techniques that involve blunt trauma, classifying them as intermediate force. Among the most common are elbow strikes, hand strikes, knee strikes and foot kicks. It is important to understand that while these techniques can be effective, they offer you no tactical advantage over your assailant. In order to strike an attacker, you have to get close enough for him to strike you. Weaponless intermediate force should be considered a secondary choice and used only when your primary intermediate weapon is inaccessible. This could happen if the subject escalates an attack so quickly that you are unable to access your baton or if you lose it while trying to defend yourself.

Besides the standard intermediate weapons and techniques, there are a couple of other force options that may be effective against an unarmed attacker. These are similar in that they may pose a similar danger of tissue damage to the subject, but they are not available to all officers.

Other Potential Intermediate Weapons

- **Chemicals**—These can be effective in repelling an attack by causing watery eyes, involuntary eye closing, difficulty in breathing and burning, prickly skin sensations. These normally disable a subject long enough to bring him into control. However, chemicals can have a serious impact on persons with respiratory problems. Proper first aid or medical treatment should be provided immediately following the use of any chemical agent, if necessary.

- **Canine**—The mere presence of a canine can have a significant psychological impact on a subject or a situation. Most unarmed subjects are not willing to tangle with a properly trained, aggressive police dog. If you are attacked, a canine can be an effective use of force by its trained actions of biting, holding and controlling a subject.

Many other types of intermediate weapons are available to law enforcement officers. These include flashlights (which should only be used in extreme circumstances) and electronic stunning devices. It is critical that all of the weapons you carry are authorized by your agency and that they are properly tested for reliability and effectiveness. In addition, you should not employ any weapon until after you have been trained in its proper use. The only exception to this rule would be if you are faced with a deadly assault and are attempting to defend yourself or another person from serious bodily injury or death. In a situation such as that, any weapon or defensive technique can be used.

Questions

1. What mental condition should you be in when confronting an unarmed assailant?

2. Under what circumstances should an unarmed assailant be re-classified as an armed assailant?

3. What are the proper steps for giving verbal commands?

4. What is meant by showing force? How is that different from using force?

5. What are the reasons why you should show force?

6. What situational assessments should you make when confronted with an unarmed threat?

7. What is the highest level of force that can be used against an unarmed attacker?

8. What weapons are authorized by your agency to be carried as intermediate weapons? What steps must you take before using any one of them?

⋘ 8 ⋙

Reacting to an
Armed Assailant

Objectives

After completing this chapter, you will be able to

- *Adopt the proper "survival" mental condition*
- *Outline the options for facing a threat by an armed assailant*
- *Detail the components of reasonable warnings*
- *Explain the importance and reasons for showing force when threatened by an armed subject*
- *Identify the circumstances that reasonably call for taking survival action*

A subject is an armed assailant when he uses a weapon to threaten or attack you or another person. Any armed confrontation can be life-threatening; you must be in the survival mode.

Officer Reaction to Armed Threat

An armed assailant is in a threatening mode when he resists custody by displaying a weapon. The threat of violence by an armed assailant is a criminal act that justifies an arrest. However, the subject's possession of a weapon results in a much more serious situation; it makes the confrontation a potential deadly attack.

SUBJECT BEHAVIOR	COOPERATIVE	NON-COOPERATIVE	UNARMED ASSAILANT	ARMED ASSAILANT
SUBJECT'S BEHAVIORAL CUES	Submits to Directions and Custody: • COMPLIANT • RESPONSIVE • FOLLOWS DIRECTIONS	Resists Custody By: • Not Responsive to Directions • Evasive to Questions • Verbal Resistance or Body Posture • Pulling/Moving or Running Away	Resists Custody By: UNARMED THREATENING — UNARMED ATTACK — Closes Distance	Resists Custody By: ARMED THREATENING — ARMED ATTACK (Deadly Assault) — Closes Distance
CRIMINAL ACTIVITY CUES		Unknown Threat	Type of Criminal Activity — Investigating	High Risk Activity
OFFICER MENTAL CONDITION	ALERT	CONTROL	ACTIVE	SURVIVAL

OFFICER'S ACTIONS	Verbal Directions	Verbal Persuasion	Verbal Commands	Verbal Warnings	Survival Action
		EMPTY HAND TECHNIQUES			
P AUTHORITY		ASSESSMENT • Custody Decision • Close Distance	SHOW FORCE	SHOW FORCE	USE FORCE
R ASSESSMENT		CONTROL BY • Escort Position	Draw Baton or Other Intermediate Weapon	Draw Firearm	Fire Weapon to Stop Attack
E CUSTODY DECISION		• Distraction Techniques	USE FORCE Use Baton or Other Intermediate Weapon		
S POSITIONING		• Compliance Holds	Assess: • Cover • Distance • Assistance • Retreat	Assess: • Cover • Distance • Assistance • Retreat	
E		• Leverage Takedowns			
N PROCEDURES		• Impact Takedowns			
C		• Chemical Agents	• Chemicals • Canine	• Canine	
E SUBMITS TO CUSTODY		FORCED CUSTODY & CONTROL PROCEDURES →			

60

A deadly attack occurs when the officer reasonably believes that the attack could result in serious bodily injury or death. As mentioned in the chapter on subject behavior cues, there are generally three types of weapons that can cause these types of injuries.

Types of Deadly Weapons

- **Firearms**—These are primarily handguns, shotguns and rifles.

- **Cutting/stabbing/hacking instruments**—Some of the most common are knives, axes, glass and all weapons having sharp edges or points.

- **Blunt trauma instruments**—These include but are not limited to baseball bats, pipes, bricks, boards and vehicles. Also, a negative disparity of force could expand the number of weapons in this category. If your assailant is much bigger or larger than you, it might be possible that his fists and feet should be considered instruments that could cause blunt trauma injuries. The same could be true if he is skilled in fighting techniques such as boxing or the martial arts or if you are faced with multiple subjects.

When reacting to an armed threat, the goal is to gain control of the assailant without having to use deadly force. A show of force or a verbal warning may be appropriate. The U.S. Supreme Court said in *Tennessee v. Garner* (a case discussed in Chapter 11) "that if a suspect threatens the officer with a weapon or there is probable cause to believe that he has committed a crime involving the infliction or threatened infliction of serious physical harm, deadly force may be used if necessary to prevent escape, and if, where feasible, some warning has been given." An effective warning could be "Police! Stop and put your weapon down! Do it now or I will shoot!" It is very direct and very clear. As an additional measure, warnings should be communicated by only one officer at the scene if other officers are present. This is the "contact and cover" concept discussed in the previous chapter; it will help prevent any confusion in the mind of the assailant as to exactly what you want him to do.

At the same time you are verbally warning the subject of the possible consequences of his actions, you should be demonstrating a "show force" posture, which the subject might view as an additional warning. As explained in the previous chapter, showing force is not the same as using force. In fact, strong verbal commands and a show of force may keep you from having to use force. And should force become necessary, showing it first will help you protect yourself and others. The reasons why showing force is important are listed below.

Reasons for Showing Force

- **Encourages the subject to comply with your orders.** The subject should be convinced that you will use the necessary force to counter an attack. Also, you should not give him the perception that he has an advantage over you. If he is showing force while you are not, he may be more likely to act against you.

- **Gives you another level at which to operate.** If you do not show force, your options are using force or not using force. Until the subject actually attacks, the first option could be excessive; the second may be less effective. The intermediate step of showing force can provide you with an opportunity to establish a tactical advantage, which may convince the subject to not escalate the incident into an attack.

- **Reduces your reaction time.** With a weapon unholstered and in a ready-to-fire position, the average speed for effective discharge of the weapon is 0.5 seconds. That is almost twice as fast as the best time recorded by an expert with a holstered gun during competition. If your weapon is holstered, you will need 2.0 to 3.0 seconds on average to fire it effectively. If you are confronted by multiple distractions at the scene, this response time may be extended by three times or more. Therefore, if you do not show force when faced with a deadly assault, you may not be able to react in time to defend yourself or another person.

Besides showing force, you should always attempt to make accurate assessments of your situation. These are the same assessments that you should make when confronted with an unarmed assailant. Once again, they will help determine the best course of action for handling a threat or an attack.

Armed Threat Situational Assessments

- **Cover**—You may be able to reduce your exposure by using on-scene objects for protection. Typical cover includes vehicles, trees and other fixed barriers when outside, and furniture and walls when inside. The use of cover can also help you with tactical deployment and approach.

- **Distance**—According to the FBI Uniform Crime Reports, the average distance of officers being shot and killed is five feet or less. Obviously, you should attempt to keep a safe distance between you and your assailant. A safe distance is usually one that gives you enough time to respond effectively should the subject initiate an attack.

- **Assistance**—Having back-up officers present may allow you more flexibility in convincing the subject to comply with your orders and submit to arrest.

- **Retreat**—It is extremely important in an armed confrontation to assess your personal safety. If you are outnumbered or outgunned, good judgment may dictate that you should attempt to disengage from the scene until a safe response can be planned. You should remember, however, that retreating or withdrawing to a more defensible position may not be a proper tactic if it allows the subject to escape the scene and pose a threat to others.

Officer Reaction to Armed Attack

Just like with an unarmed assault, a subject crosses over the line from armed threatening to armed attack when he closes distance by moving toward you with a weapon. When the subject has a firearm that you believe to be within its effective range, the attack is initiated when he begins to move the weapon in your direction. Once the gun is in position to fire, the attack will be completed as the point of zero reaction time has occurred; you will not be able to stop the subject from discharging his weapon.

An assailant armed with a cutting, stabbing, hacking or blunt trauma weapon in a high intensity attack can cover a distance of approximately 21 to 30 feet in about 1.5 seconds. This is also the minimum amount of time required to process the attack information and respond effectively if you have not drawn your firearm to a "show force" position. (This demonstrates the need to show force when confronted by armed, threatening subjects.) The point in which you will not be able to take an action to repel an attack ranges from 6 to 15 feet, depending upon the speed or intensity with which the subject is moving towards you.

If you are attacked by an armed assailant, you should **take survival action**, using any reasonable force necessary to defend yourself. In most armed attack situations, this requires the firing of your weapon. It should be noted, however, that if you are justified in using your firearm to stop a deadly attack, you are legally authorized to use any available weapon or defensive technique to defend yourself. In many situations, an armed attack can happen so quickly that your only defense option is to use an empty-hand technique or an intermediate weapon. The actions that you take will be evaluated based on the standard of reasonableness, the facts of the incident and your state of mind at the time of the attack.

If you do use your firearm, it is important to remember that your goal is to stop the actions of your attacker, not to kill him. Your agency should provide you with clear directives about the tactics for using your firearm and will provide proper training on these techniques.

There are a couple of other issues to keep in mind regarding taking survival action. First, as mentioned earlier, the case of *Tennessee v. Garner* established a requirement that, "where feasible," a warning should be given before firing your weapon. When an officer is forced to take a survival action and fire a weapon to stop an attack, he or she may not have time to give a verbal warning. The reason is that it is impossible to hold your breath (a fundamental of shooting) and verbalize at the same time. So if an armed attack happens so quickly that you must immediately fire your weapon to defend yourself and stop the attack, it will be physically impossible to verbally warn the attacker.

Second, in the course of defending yourself from an armed attack, your response may result in a serious injury or the death of your assailant. As long as you have responded within the parameters outlined in the Reactive Control Model, your response should be considered reasonable, lawful and consistent with your department's policies and procedures.

Questions

1. What mental condition should you be in when confronting an armed assailant?

2. What steps should you use to counter an armed threat?

4. What are the components of a verbal warning?

5. What are the reasons for showing force when confronting an armed assailant?

6. What situational assessments should you make when faced with an armed threat?

7. What is meant by "taking survival action?" When would such a response be considered reasonable?

8. What is your goal when attacked by an armed assailant? What are your agency's procedures for achieving this goal?

⋙ 9 ⋘

Post-Incident Review

Objectives

After completing this chapter, you will be able to

- *Explain why the Reactive Control Model is a valuable post-incident tool*
- *Identify the post-incident uses of the model, both for the line officer and the agency*
- *Use the model to demonstrate the proper method for conducting a review*

Any use-of-force response will be evaluated using the standard of reasonableness. Because the Reactive Control Model is based on the legal standard of reasonableness and conforms to training standards accepted throughout the United States, it provides a framework for clearly documenting and explaining your actions. As such, the model is just as effective after an incident is over as it was while events were unfolding.

Ways in which the Model Can Be Used

Any use of force incident will likely be reviewed by your supervisor and may undergo examination by a police review board. Incidents of a serious nature may also be subject to review by the district or prosecuting attorney's office and, in some cases, subject to civil examination. It is imperative that you accurately document the facts of the incident and your state of mind at the time you were compelled to use force. The model helps you do this. As such, it has a variety of post-incident uses.

Post Incident Uses by a Line Officer

• **Report writing**—The model serves as an excellent tool for writing comprehensive, detailed reports. It helps you focus on the critical aspects of the incident and gives you a logical starting point. You should begin by stating the criminal activity cues, detailing the type of incident that you were investigating and any anticipated behaviors that might be associated with this type of investigation. You should then detail the specific types of subject cues, including the behaviors you witnessed when you initially encountered the subject as well as his behaviors demonstrated throughout the incident. From this, you can document the specific actions you took, including any escalations due to increased resistance or de-escalations resulting from the subject's decision to cooperate. Of course, you must also document the probable cause for the arrest in your report.

• **Self-evaluation**—You can also use the model as an evaluation tool to determine whether the force used was balanced, less effective or excessive. Knowing that your response was appropriate given the subject's behavior will reinforce your decision and increase your confidence. On the other hand, if you find you used a level of force that was higher or lower than what was appropriate, that knowledge will help you make the proper decision when confronted with a similar situation in the future.

• **Grand jury and courtroom testimony**—By providing a visual depiction of your decision-making process, the model is a very effective tool for testifying in court.

You can use the model to plot subject behavioral cues and criminal activity cues and then show how they led to your response decision. This will demonstrate to the judge and jurors that you are well trained and know how to make a reasonable, proper use-of-force decision.

The Reactive Control Model has many uses for the agency, as well. A few of them are listed below.

Post Incident Uses by an Agency

- **Supervisory review**—The model serves as an excellent tool for evaluating an officer's response and tactics in a particular incident. By checking whether the response lined up with the subject behavior cues, a supervisor can determine immediately whether it was in line with departmental policy or whether the force used was below optimum or excessive. This information can then be used to reinforce the officer's decision-making skills or it can be used to demonstrate how those skills can be improved.

- **Management analysis**—The model can also be used by law enforcement executives and commanders to analyze use-of-force tactics and to track trends in the department. This analysis can point to training needs and can reveal the need for policy updates or revisions.

- **Internal affairs investigations**—The model can be effectively used by internal affairs officers to investigate allegations of excessive force. After reviewing all reports and interviewing all witnesses and persons involved, internal affairs investigators can then use the model to indicate the actions of both the subject and the officer. This aspect is important because it provides an objective criterion for evaluation, one that is based on department policy and training. Too often in the past, there have been complaints from officers that internal affairs investigators did not understand use-of-force training or did not apply what was taught in training when conducting their investigations. Use of the Reactive Control Model should improve the ability of internal affairs investigators to objectively determine whether proper and reasonable force was used.

Conducting a Review

Conducting a review using the RCM is a fairly simple process. The first step is to plot the behavioral cues demonstrated by a subject and the response that you took. Then all you need to do is draw a line between them.

If the line is perpendicular, (straight up and down) then the subject behavior cues lines up perfectly with your use-of-force response. The conclusion then is that the response was **balanced**; your decision was the most appropriate given the situation.

One thing to keep in mind here is that a straight line points to the most effective response, but it is not the only acceptable or reasonable response. When lining up the subject behavioral cues with officer reaction, you can use any level of force up to that line. In the illustration provided, any use-of-force response to the left of the line would be considered reasonable. For instance, if an unarmed subject threatens you, you can defend yourself by using a leverage takedown to bring him under control. Based on the Reactive Control Model, this technique is considered potentially less effective. So while it would not be the best technique for the situation, it would still be a reasonable use of force.

On the other hand, any use-of-force response to the right of the line could be considered excessive. As such, while you can draw a baton as a "show force" measure when confronted with an unarmed assailant, you should not use the baton unless the subject attacks you.

SUBJECT BEHAVIOR	COOPERATIVE	NON-COOPERATIVE	UNARMED ASSAILANT		ARMED ASSAILANT	
SUBJECT'S BEHAVIORAL CUES	Submits to Directions and Custody: • COMPLIANT • RESPONSIVE • FOLLOWS DIRECTIONS	Resists Custody By: • Not Responsive to Directions • Evasive to Questions • Verbal Resistance or Body Posture • Pulling/Moving or Running Away	Resists Custody By: UNARMED THREATENING	UNARMED ATTACK Closes Distance	Resists Custody By: ARMED THREATENING	ARMED ATTACK (Deadly Assault) Closes Distance
CRIMINAL ACTIVITY CUES	Unknown Threat	Type of Criminal Activity Investigating			High Risk Activity	
OFFICER MENTAL CONDITION	ALERT	CONTROL	ACTIVE		SURVIVAL	
OFFICER'S ACTIONS	Verbal Directions	Verbal Persuasion	Verbal Commands		Verbal Warnings	Survival Action
		EMPTY HAND TECHNIQUES ASSESSMENT CONTROL BY	SHOW FORCE / USE FORCE Draw Baton or Other Intermediate Weapon / Use Baton or Other Intermediate Weapon Assess: • Cover • Distance • Assistance • Retreat	• Chemicals • Canine	SHOW FORCE / USE FORCE Draw Firearm / Fire Weapon to Stop Attack Assess: • Cover • Distance • Assistance • Retreat	

OFFICER'S ACTIONS (P R E S E N C E):
- • AUTHORITY
- • ASSESSMENT
- • CUSTODY DECISION
- • POSITIONING
- • PROCEDURES

CONTROL BY:
- • Custody Decision
- • Close Distance
- • Escort Position
- • Distraction Techniques
- • Compliance Holds
- • Leverage Takedowns
- • Impact Takedowns

SUBMITS TO CUSTODY ← ← ← FORCED CUSTODY → ← ← FORCED CUSTODY & CONTROL PROCEDURES → → → →
• Chemical Agents → • Canine

A Balanced Response

If the line drawn from plotting the subject's behavior cues and your response slants either left or right, you can conclude that your decision was not balanced. Should the line slant to the left (going from top to bottom), the force you used should be considered less effective. This is illustrated on the following page.

If you use force that is less than effective or less than balanced, you should provide specific reasons why you chose that level of response. Perhaps, given the dynamics of the confrontation, a lower level of control may have been the only option available. An armed attack can happen so quickly that the only available response is an empty hand technique. As stated before, any technique or instrument that you are trained in and authorized to use at lower levels can be used when a subject's cues indicate a higher level of response. If you are justified in using your firearm to stop a deadly attack, it is only reasonable that you would be legally authorized to use any available weapon or defensive technique to stop a deadly assault.

In some cases, officers have chosen to use potentially ineffective force for any number of reasons. However, there are a couple of things that you should keep in mind if you are ever considering such a response. First, our research has shown that a less than optimum response is often ineffective in bringing a subject under control. Therefore, an ineffective response could lead to you or someone else being injured. Second, a less than optimum response may allow the subject to escalate to a higher level of resistance or violence, thereby forcing you to escalate your response. So while a lower level response may result in a positive resolution, you should be aware of the risks involved when you chose to use it.

Should the line slant to the right (going from top to bottom), the force used would be considered **excessive and unreasonable**. (See illustration on page 74.) You will need to account for the reason why that happened.

Such a situation could be considered justified in two possible circumstances: an escalation in threat or a negative disparity of force. Using the example of the illustration shown, a noncooperative subject's active resistance could very quickly esca-

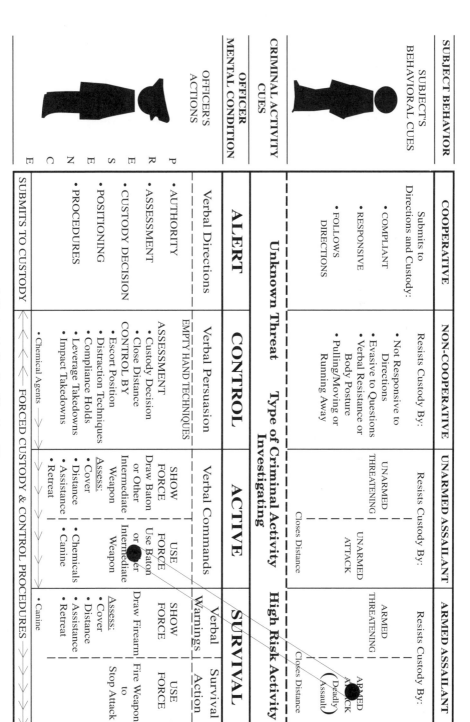

SUBJECT BEHAVIOR	COOPERATIVE	NON-COOPERATIVE	UNARMED ASSAILANT	ARMED ASSAILANT
SUBJECT'S BEHAVIORAL CUES	Submits to Directions and Custody: • COMPLIANT • RESPONSIVE • FOLLOWS DIRECTIONS	Resists Custody By: • Not Responsive to Directions • Evasive to Questions • Verbal Resistance or Body Posture • Pulling/Moving or Running Away	Resists Custody By: UNARMED THREATENING / UNARMED ATTACK — Closes Distance	Resists Custody By: ARMED THREATENING / ARMED ATTACK (Deadly Assault) — Closes Distance
CRIMINAL ACTIVITY CUES	Unknown Threat	Type of Criminal Activity Investigating	High Risk Activity	
OFFICER MENTAL CONDITION	ALERT	CONTROL	ACTIVE	SURVIVAL
OFFICER'S ACTIONS	Verbal Directions	Verbal Persuasion	Verbal Commands	Verbal Warnings / Survival Action

OFFICER'S ACTIONS (detail):

ALERT — Verbal Directions

CONTROL — Verbal Persuasion
EMPTY HAND TECHNIQUES
ASSESSMENT • Custody Decision • Close Distance
CONTROL BY • Escort Position • Distraction Techniques • Compliance Holds • Leverage Takedowns • Impact Takedowns

ACTIVE — Verbal Commands
SHOW FORCE Draw Baton or Other Intermediate Weapon
Assess: • Cover • Distance • Assistance • Canine
USE FORCE Use Baton or other Intermediate Weapon • Chemicals • Canine

SURVIVAL — Verbal Warnings
SHOW FORCE Draw Firearm
Assess: • Cover • Distance • Assistance • Retreat
Survival Action USE FORCE Fire Weapon to Stop Attack

P R E S E N C E
• AUTHORITY
• ASSESSMENT
• CUSTODY DECISION
• POSITIONING
• PROCEDURES

SUBMITS TO CUSTODY ← • Chemical Agents → FORCED CUSTODY & CONTROL PROCEDURES →

A Potentially Ineffective Response

SUBJECT BEHAVIOR	COOPERATIVE	NON-COOPERATIVE	UNARMED ASSAILANT	ARMED ASSAILANT
SUBJECT'S BEHAVIORAL CUES	Submits to Directions and Custody: • COMPLIANT • RESPONSIVE • FOLLOWS DIRECTIONS	Resists Custody By: • Not Responsive to Directions • Evasive Questions • Verbal Resistance or Body Posture • Pulling/Moving or Running Away	Resists Custody By: UNARMED THREATENING — UNARMED ATTACK Closes Distance	Resists Custody By: ARMED THREATENING — ARMED ATTACK (Deadly Assault) Closes Distance
CRIMINAL ACTIVITY CUES	Unknown Threat	Type of Criminal Activity Investigating		High Risk Activity
OFFICER MENTAL CONDITION	ALERT	CONTROL	ACTIVE	SURVIVAL

OFFICER'S ACTIONS	Verbal Directions
	
	P • AUTHORITY
	R • ASSESSMENT
	E • CUSTODY DECISION
	S • POSITIONING
	E • PROCEDURES
	N
	C
	E
		Verbal Persuasion
		
		EMPTY HAND TECHNIQUES
		ASSESSMENT
		• Custody Decision
		• Close Distance
		CONTROL BY
		• Escort Position
		• Distraction Techniques
		• Compliance Holds
		• Leverage Takedowns
		• Impact Takedowns
			Verbal Commands
			       USE FORCE
			SHOW FORCE
			Draw Baton or Other Intermediate Weapon
			Assess:
			• Cover
			• Distance
			• Assistance
			• Retreat
				Verbal Warnings Survival Action
				      USE FORCE
				SHOW FORCE
				Draw Firearm — Fire Weapon to Stop Attack
				Assess:
				• Cover
				• Distance
				• Assistance
				• Retreat

Use Baton or Other Intermediate Weapon

• Chemicals • Canine

• Chemical Agents →

• Canine

SUBMITS TO CUSTODY   ← FORCED CUSTODY & CONTROL PROCEDURES →

An Excessive and Unreasonable Response

late to the point of being an unarmed attack. If that occurred, you should reclassify the subject behavior cues to demonstrate the higher level of threat. You should also do the same if the subject or subjects demonstrate a distinct advantage over you due to their size, skill or numbers. As long as the higher level of threat lines up with your response, you can then show that the level of force that you used was appropriate and reasonable.

However, you must keep in mind that an escalation in threat or a negative disparity of force does not authorize you to use just any level of force that you choose. Your response must still be based on the specific officer response levels as shown in the Reactive Control Model. As an example, the only time that it is consider reasonable to fire your weapon to stop an attack is when you truly believe that the attack could result in a deadly assault of a citizen, another officer or you.

Questions

1. Why is the Reactive Control Model a valuable post-incident tool?

2. How can you use the model for report writing?

3. How can the model be effectively used for testifying in court or before a grand jury?

4. In what ways can an agency use the model after an incident is over?

5. How should the model be used for a post-incident review? What must occur for you to conclude that your response was balance? What would indicate a potentially ineffective response? What would indicate an excessive or unreasonable response?

6. What are the dangers of selecting a potentially ineffective level of response?

7. Under what circumstances could a seemingly excessive response be shown to be balanced and reasonable?

8. Based on the facts of an incident that you have been involved in, conduct a mock review using the Reactive Control Model.

❦ PART FOUR ❦

Legal Issues

❧ 10 ❧

Legal Standards

Objectives

After completing this chapter you will be able to:

- *Identify the primary standards that govern the use of force*
- *Explain why policy is important for both administrators and line officers*
- *Identify how a violation of established standards can lead to litigation or other sanctions*

While the Reactive Control Model helps you make reasonable and appropriate decisions, it is also important that you understand the legal standards that apply to the use of force. When you know the rules, you are more likely to stay within them.

The Primary Standards

There are a number of standards throughout the country that impact the use of force, but there are three that carry the most weight in court. These are the primary standards of what type of force can be used as well as when and how it can be applied.

Primary Standards for the Use of Force

- **The United States Constitution**—Sets the broad standards defining the rights of all individuals within the United States, be they citizens or not.

- **State statutes**—Define the penal code and code of criminal procedures that are acceptable within the boundaries of each state. Standards can be created by state constitutions, as well.

- **Agency policy**—Outlines the proper procedures for carrying out your duties. A policy must be consistent and stay within the bounds of the other legal standards. A policy can be more limiting than the U.S. Constitution and state statutes but cannot be more permissive.

Standards Set by the U.S. Constitution

When it comes to the U.S. Constitution, there are several amendments that have a significant impact on the use of force. The Eighth Amendment protects people from cruel and unusual punishment. As such, it applies to actions that occur after a person has been found guilty of a crime. The Fourteenth Amendment, guaranteeing that no person shall be denied the right of life, liberty or property without due process of law, used to be the key determinant of the standards of force used by law enforcement officers. That changed in 1989 when the Supreme Court decided the case of *Graham v. Connor*. The facts in that case are as follows:

Graham, a diabetic, asked a friend to drive him to a convenience store to buy some orange juice to counteract an insulin reaction. When he got to the store, he saw a number of people ahead of him, so he quickly left and asked his friend to drive him to another friend's house.

Officer Connor, having seen Graham enter and leave hurriedly, became suspicious and stopped the car. He ordered Graham and his friend to wait while he checked out what had happened back at the store. When Officer Connor returned to his patrol car to call for backup assistance, Graham got out of the car, ran around it twice and finally sat down on the curb where he passed out.

When backup officers arrived on the scene, one of them rolled Graham over on the sidewalk and cuffed his hands tightly behind his back, ignoring his friend's pleas to get Graham some sugar. Several officers then lifted Graham up from behind, carried him over to his friend's car and placed him face down on its hood.

Regaining consciousness, Graham asked the officers to check his wallet for a diabetic identification card that he carried. In response, one of the officers told him to "shut up" and shoved his face down against the hood of the car. Four officers then grabbed Graham and threw him head-first into the police car. A friend of Graham's brought some orange juice to the car, but the officers refused to let Graham have it.

Finally, Officer Connor received a report that Graham had done nothing wrong at the convenience store. The officers then drove him home and released him.

During his encounter with the police, Graham sustained a broken foot, cuts on his wrists, a bruised forehead and an injured shoulder. He also claimed to have developed a loud ringing in his right ear. He commenced an action against the officers involved in the incident, alleging that they violated his right to due process guaranteed under the Fourteenth Amendment when they used excessive force in making the investigative stop.

The significant aspect of the *Graham v. Connor* decision is that it set the Fourth Amendment to the U.S. Constitution as the established standard for all use of force cases in federal court. The Fourth Amendment guarantees all persons the right to be free from unreasonable seizures. The Supreme Court stated that an arrest or an investigative stop is a seizure, so any excessive force claim arising from a seizure should be characterized as one invoking the protection of the Fourth Amendment.

What this means is that a judge or jury should not evaluate the conduct of an officer based on whether a person's right to due process was denied. Instead, the officer's conduct should be measured using the concept of **objective reasonableness**. Officers on the street have to make split-second life or death decisions.

Therefore, their actions "must be judged from the perspective of a reasonable officer on the scene, not the 20/20 vision of hindsight." In other words, the Supreme Court said that the determining factor in establishing reasonableness should be based on what any reasonable officer would think or do if confronted with the exact same facts or circumstances. This requires officers to pay careful attention to the facts and circumstances of each particular case, including the severity of the crime at issue; whether the suspect poses an immediate threat to the officer or others; and whether he is actively resisting arrest or attempting to evade arrest by flight.

Standards Created by State Statute or Law

States have created their own standards relating to the use of force by peace officers. These standards generally model the U.S. Constitution. They can be more restrictive but not more permissive. States also establish standards through their statutory laws which govern criminal and civil actions. Some states outline use-of-force guidelines for law enforcement officers in statute. Others only address the use of deadly force in justifiable homicide statutes. State laws also govern torts or civil actions, creating potential liability for law enforcement officers actions in specific situations.

Standards Created by Policy

The policies of a law enforcement agency are general guidelines which direct the actions and behaviors of its officers. By establishing what an officer's responsibilities are, specific standards are created. In many cases, agencies will take the broad duties created by the constitution, made narrower by state statute or local ordinance and then tailor them to fit the needs of their individual communities.

Failure to have a meaningful policy may subject an agency to liability, even in cases where administrators may have provided some guidance. It is up to your department to outline a clear and comprehensive policy that can withstand a challenge in court. Once a policy is set, the agency must provide proper training to implement it.

As a law enforcement officer, you must completely understand and abide by your agency's policy on the use of force. Any breach of a standard created by policy may subject an officer to the potential for administrative sanctions as well as legal action. If a plaintiff claims that he was injured because you failed to follow your agency's policy, you may be held directly liable in civil action. At the same time, depending upon the nature of the alleged misconduct, you may also be criminally prosecuted.

One area that is often overlooked is the **informal policy** of an agency. An agency may have a very good written policy and procedure for an area of operations, but what actually occurs in the field may be quite different. If the practice is allowed to continue and the supervisors knew or should have known that it was occurring, then that practice becomes the informal policy of the agency, regardless of what the written policy is. The caution here is that informal policies are often outside the scope of what is acceptable by the standards of the profession and what is allowed by law.

Violations of Standards

Any violation of the legal standards discussed in this chapter could be considered a tort. A tort is a wrong of a civil nature that can result in a lawsuit brought by an individual who is harmed by the wrong. There are several categories.

One is the **constitutional tort**, known as such because it deals with protection guaranteed to the people by the U. S. Constitution. If an individual believes that his constitutional rights have been violated, he can bring an action against those responsible for that violation by way of Title 42 of the United States Code, Section 1983 (42 USC 1983).

Section 1983 states that "every person who, under color of any statute, ordinance, regulation, custom, or usage, of any state or territory or the District of Columbia, subjects, or causes to be subjected, any citizen of the United States or other person within the jurisdiction thereof to the deprivation of any rights, privileges, or immunities secured by the constitution and laws, shall be liable to the party injured in an action at law, suit in equity, or other proper proceedings for redress." In plain language, this statute provides civil remedies for a person deprived of any U.S. Constitutional right or privilege by another person who is acting under the color of law, which includes law enforcement officers.

Congress enacted Section 1983 in 1871. Prior to that, a person could not sue state officials or people acting under the color of state law in federal court if the actions of the state violated his constitutional rights. He could sue in state court, but Congress did not believe there was enough protection of federal rights there. In effect, a person could be denied constitutional rights, depending upon how a state court interpreted the U.S. Constitution. Congress felt that the Constitution and its Amendments did not mean much unless a person had a way to take advantage of their benefits. So with the passage of Section 1983, any deprivation of a federal civil right or privilege is compensable by law in federal court.

Another type of tort is the **negligence tort**. Based on the standards mentioned earlier, law enforcement officers have duties to the people they have sworn to protect. If an officer's conduct results in a failure to exercise due care to a person to whom a duty is owed, that person can file a suit against the officer, even if the harm was unintended. The level of liability that the officer is exposed to will be determined by the risk posed by his actions. If the risks were great, his conduct may be characterized as reckless or wanton.

Agencies are subject to negligence claims, as well. If an agency does not teach, train, direct, supervise and discipline its personnel properly in the use of force, an injured plaintiff or a deceased plaintiff's estate can sue the agency for negligence, claiming that the department did not fulfill its duty to the plaintiff.

A higher level liability is the **intentional tort**. While negligence is liability stemming from harm that a person did not mean to cause, an intentional tort is a wrong that an officer did on purpose. Intentional torts include actions such as assault and battery, false arrest and imprisonment, malicious prosecution and intentional infliction of emotional distress.

The distinction between intentional actions and negligence is a matter of degree. However, the courts seem to have drawn the line between them. An officer's actions are negligent when the dangers posed by his conduct were foreseeable risks that a reasonable person would have avoided. In other words, he should have known what could happen and taken a different course. His actions can be classified as intentional when the dangers posed by his conduct were a substantial certainty. He knew what the risks were and what the probable outcome would be, yet he took the action anyway.

The last general category of tort is that of **strict liability**. The mere occurrence of certain behavior, generally extremely hazardous conduct, will create legal liability to anyone injured. Under strict liability, an officer can be held liable for his actions, no matter if they were intentional or the result of negligence.

Whenever an injured party feels that his injury was the result of law enforcement activity, the conduct of the officers involved will be measured against the standards that were mentioned earlier to determine whether an actionable cause may exist. To do this, the potential plaintiff and his attorney will consider a couple of questions. First, was the conduct inconsistent with applicable constitutional law, state law, agency policy, training, etc.? Second, does it rise to the level of tort liability? If they conclude that the answer to both is "yes," a lawsuit will likely be filed.

Questions

1. What are the primary standards guiding the use of force?

2. What standard did the Supreme Court establish in *Graham v. Connor* that must be used when evaluating a plaintiff's claim

of excessive use of force?

3. What laws in your state constitution or created by state statutes apply to the use of force in your state?

4. How do the standards created by agency policy compare to the standards created by the U. S. Constitution and state statutes?

5. What is your agency's policy on the use of force?

6. What is meant by the term "the informal policy" of an agency? Why are informal policies dangerous?

7. What is a tort?

8. Explain what Section 1983 is. How does it impact law enforcement activities?

9. What is the difference between a negligence tort and an intentional tort?

⋖ 11 ⋗

Determining Reasonable Force

Objectives

After completing this chapter, you will be able to

- *Understand why probable cause is required prior to making any arrest*
- *Understand the difference between reasonable suspicion and probable cause*
- *Understand the legal requirements that guide the use of deadly force by a peace officer*

The use of force standards discussed in Chapter 10 state that force can be used as long as it is objectively reasonable. However, they do not actually define reasonable force. This chapter addresses that issue.

Probable Cause

In order to arrest someone, you must first have authority to do so. That authority may be in the form of a court order, a warrant, extradition papers or your own decision made in the field. When you yourself make the determination that a person should be arrested, that decision must be based on the standard of probable cause. **Probable cause is defined as a combination of facts or apparent facts that would lead a person of reasonable caution to believe that a subject has committed, is currently committing, or is about to commit a crime.** It is more than mere suspicion but far less than the evidence sufficient to justify a conviction. Examples of factors that might be used to establish probable cause include the following:

- Commits an illegal act that you witness
- Suspicious conduct
- Known criminal record
- Evidence in plain view
- Resistance to officers
- Evasive answers or unreasonable explanations
- Admissions or confessions
- Identification of suspects by witnesses
- Hearsay evidence, such as from an informant

A few other things need to be mentioned about probable cause. First, your experience as a law enforcement officer will play a role. The more knowledge and training you have, the more likely a court will consider your observations and conclusions of a situation to be valid and reasonable.

In addition, the facts that led you to your conclusions do not necessarily have to be true. You just have to believe they are true. As long as this belief is reasonable, probable cause can be established. However, if you have probable cause to arrest someone but then discover additional facts indicating that the original probable cause no longer exists, the subject must be released.

As for reasonable force, you have the authority to overcome resistance to a lawful arrest or stop a criminal act. If you have established probable cause for a lawful arrest and the subject resists, you are allowed to use force to establish control and custody of the individual. It is important to note that any force used must be appropriate for the level of resistance that you encounter or the seriousness of the crime committed. And, of course, without probable cause for an arrest, any level of force used against a person could be considered unlawful.

One last point needs to be made about making an arrest decision. While probable cause must be established before an arrest can be made, you are authorized to stop and investigate a subject based on a lower standard known as **reasonable suspi-**

cion. Reasonable suspicion is defined as articulable facts that would lead an experienced law enforcement officer to believe that a person may have or may be about to commit a crime. Some examples that provide an officer with reasonable suspicion are:

- **What type of crime is suspected?** The more serious the crime, the more compelling the need to investigate quickly.
- **Where and when is contact made?** The time and place are significant.
- **What exactly is the suspect doing?** Many actions by themselves will trigger a desire to investigate.

If you have reasonable suspicion, you may investigate to establish probable cause. If, as previously discussed, probable cause can be established, you may arrest the subject. If it cannot, the subject must be released.

Deadly Force

Human rights and the protection of our citizens is the cornerstone of our democracy. Because our society places such a high value on human life and the rights of citizens, the decision to use deadly force is the most serious decision that you will ever make. You have the authority to use deadly force in the lawful performance of your duties but only under very strict guidelines. In 1985, the U. S. Supreme Court set the standard for police use of deadly force in deciding the case of *Tennessee v. Garner*. The facts of the case are as follows:

One night two Memphis police officers answered a "prowler inside" call. When they arrived on the scene, they encountered a woman gesturing towards the house next door, saying that she had heard glass breaking. While one officer notified the dispatch that they were on the scene, the other officer went around to the back of the house in question. He heard a door slam and saw someone run across the backyard to a six-foot chain-link fence. That person was later identified as 15-year-old Edward Garner.

Using a flashlight, the police officer got a good look at Garner. The officer saw no weapon and later stated that he was "reasonably certain" that the suspect was unarmed. While Garner was crouched at the base of the fence, the officer ordered him to stop. As the officer took a few steps towards him, Garner began to climb over the fence. Convinced that Garner would get away if he made it over the fence, the officer shot him. Garner was taken by ambulance to a hospital where he died. Ten dollars and a purse taken from the house were found on his body.

By using deadly force to prevent the escape, the officer was acting in accordance with Tennessee statute. It stated that an officer could use any force necessary to effect an arrest if a subject attempted to flee or forcibly resisted. The agency policy was slightly more restrictive than the statute but still allowed the use of deadly force in cases of burglary.

However, the Supreme Court ruled that the law and policy were not reasonable. The court stated that it is not constitutionally reasonable for a peace officer to use deadly force to stop a fleeing suspect unless the officer has probable cause to believe that the suspect poses a serious threat of physical harm to the officer or someone else. In other words, unless you believe the suspect could cause serious bodily harm to you or someone else, you cannot use deadly force to stop him.

This ruling does not apply just to suspects in flight. Anytime a subject commences a deadly attack against you, it would be objectively reasonable for you to defend yourself using any means available. The same would be true if a subject places other people in imminent jeopardy. For instance, if an armed subject has taken hostages and threatens or uses deadly violence against them, a decision by peace officers to apply deadly force to stop the hostage-taker would likely be judged reasonable.

There are a couple of important considerations to keep in mind about the *Garner* decision. First, you do not actually have to be in a life-threatening situation; you just have to believe that you are in a life-threatening situation. As long as this belief is based on probable cause, using deadly force to protect yourself or others should be judged reasonable.

Second, the Court said that, whenever feasible, a peace officer should give a warning before using deadly force. What this means is that, if the situation allows, you should warn the subject by any means available of the consequences of his actions.

Using the Legal Information

Having read these chapters on the legal aspects of the use of force, you may be wondering how to use all of this information. How can you use the force you are authorized to use to serve your community and to protect your safety and the safety of others, all the while also protecting yourself from lawsuits? The answer is simple: Follow the Reactive Control Model.

The Reactive Control Model (RCM) takes into account the legal standards and the case law on reasonable force handed down by the U.S. Supreme Court. It instructs you on how to make a response decision based on a subject's specific behaviors as well as the severity of his criminal activity. The model defines what is an appropriate use-of-force response by a law enforcement officer for virtually any situation that you might encounter. As such, the RCM will guide you in making the right decisions. These are the ones that can stand scrutiny and allow us to protect and serve in the finest tradition of the law enforcement profession. They are also the decisions that enable us to maintain the respect of the community, the department, our fellow officers and, most importantly, ourselves.

Questions

1. What is probable cause? How does it apply to a lawful arrest? How does it apply to the reasonable use of force?

2. How does reasonable suspicion differ from probable cause?

3. What standard regarding the use of deadly force was established by the U. S. Supreme Court in *Tennessee v. Garner?*

4. What important considerations must be kept in mind regarding the use of deadly force standard established by *Tennessee v. Garner*?

Glossary

Contact and cover—A technique that is used in situations where there are multiple officers and usually a single subject. One officer is designated as the contact officer and controls all communications with the subject; the back-up officers serve as cover officers and tactically take positions to ensure the safety of the contact officer and others at the scene.

Cue—An action taken by a subject or information available to an officer that indicates a conditioned or trained response.

Deadly attack—An assault on a person with or without weapons in which the person under attack believes that the attack has the potential for causing serious bodily injury or death.

Deadly weapon—An instrument or object that can be used to cause serious bodily injury or death. The three general categories of deadly weapons are firearms, blunt trauma instruments and cutting, stabbing and hacking instruments.

Disparity of force—An unequal advantage of one person or group of individuals over another, which is gained through muscular strength, specialized training or the possession of certain types of weapons. Disparity can also occur through the use of drugs or alcohol which can temporarily enhance a person's physical strength and increase their threshold of pain.

Effective range—The distance in which a weapon can be used in an attack to cause serious bodily injury or death. For example, a person with a knife who is 50 feet away is normally not within the effective range of the weapon. On the hand, a person with a handgun who is 50 feet way is normally within the effective range of the weapon.

Empty hand techniques—Defensive tactics in which no weapons are used by an officer. These tactics are normally used to control a resistant, non-cooperative subject. They do not include blunt trauma techniques such as kicks, punches, etc.

Extension of violence—This frequently occurs when a person is threatening to commit or is committing a crime (in some instances, a suicide attempt), and another person attempts to intervene to control the behavior. The person threatening or committing the crime often redirects or extends their attention or attack to the intervening party. The extension of violence is normally found in situations in which an officer arrives at a scene and the violence or threat of violence is then directed toward the officer.

Informal policy—A course of action, guideline or procedure that is usually followed in certain situations but which is not formally recognized as a documented policy or approved by the agency. It may or may not comply with accepted standards.

Intensity of attack—The speed or force in which a subject physically moves when committing an attack. The speed or force in which a subject closes distance to the intended target can range from the movement of a handgun to a shooting position or it may occur when a subject with a knife is walking or running toward an officer.

Level of threat—An officer's assessment of a subject's behavior gained from observation, training, personal knowledge or experience in which the officer can mentally and physically prepare for the potential or seriousness of danger.

Mental condition—An officer's mental preparation which is indexed from observation, personal experience or information, to respond reasonably and properly to a subject's behavior.

Negative disparity of force—This occurs when a subject or subjects have the physical and/or psychological advantage over an officer or officers. The advantage can be gained through the number of subjects at the scene and through the muscular strength, specialized training or the possession of certain types of weapons displayed by a subject. A negative disparity of force can also occur when a subject or subjects have used certain types of drugs or alcohol which can increase their physical strength or increase their threshold to pain.

Performance action—The execution of a physical movement or action that is taken to avoid, repel or stop an attack.

Point of zero reaction—The point when an attacking subject reaches a distance or positions a weapon in such a manner that the officer cannot avoid, repel or take a defensive action to stop the attack. When an assailant has reached the point of zero reaction, the attack can be completed.

Policy—Something that establishes a course of action, guidelines or procedures to follow in specific situations. It is often a written document.

Positive disparity of force—This occurs when an officer or officers have the physical and/or psychological advantage over a subject or subjects. The advantage can be gained through the number of officers at the scene and through the muscular strength, specialized training or the possession of certain types of weapons carried by an officer.

Probable cause—A combination of facts or apparent facts that would lead a person of reasonable caution to believe that a subject has committed, is currently committing, or is about to commit a crime.

Reaction time—The time interval it takes an officer to perceive a threat, formulate a decision on what specific defensive action to take and initiate that action to avoid, repel or stop the attack.

Reasonable suspicion—Articulable facts that would lead an experienced law enforcement officer to believe that a person may have or may be about to commit a crime.

Serious bodily harm—An assault on a person in which the assailant's attack may cause large, gaping wound, severe internal organ damage or major bone breakage.

Show of force—The physical and/or verbal communications between an officer and a threatening subject that visually and/ or verbally conveys the action that will be taken should the subject continue his threats of violence or resistance. It is used in a law enforcement context to convince a threatening subject to comply with the lawful orders of the officer as well as to reduce the officer's reaction time should the subject initiate an attack.

Situational distractions—Actions, movements or sounds at a scene that may cause an officer's attention to be directed away from a serious or dangerous threat. These distractions can cause an officer's reaction time to be significantly increased should an attack be initiated by an assailant.

Standards—Measures that are considered to be the accepted practice or procedure, often used as a comparative guideline.

Survival action—Requires that an officer be at the highest level of mental preparation and take an immediate defensive action which is normally the firing of his or her weapon to stop the assailant's deadly attack. Usually an officer will be unable to verbally communicate with an assailant when taking a survival action, due to the physiological requirement of interrupting and stopping their breathing while firing a firearem.

Index

About the Authors

Thomas T. Gillespie

Tom Gillespie began his law enforcement career in 1970 in Detroit, Michigan. He has served as a Municipal Police Chief, City Manager, New Mexico State Department of Public Safety Training Director and Director of the New Mexico Attorney General's Investigations Division. Since 1987, he has operated Criminal Justice Training & Consulting Services which provides training in areas such as use of force, critical incident management and police involved shooting programs throughout the United States and abroad. Mr. Gillespie also provides expert witness case review, evaluation and testimony in civil actions involving police training, supervision, use of force, false arrest and personnel actions. He has authored numerous articles in the law enforcement and critical incident management fields.

Darrel G. Hart

Darrel Hart is the Director of the Training and Recruiting Division of the New Mexico Department of Public Safety. He is a certified instructor in firearms, defensive tactics, custody control, use of force, executive development, fitness training, officer survival, emergency vehicle operations, radar operations, dignitary protection and management and supervision. He has taught as an adjunct faculty member for Northwestern University's School of Police Staff and Command, the Northern New Mexico Community College and the Santa Fe Community College. Mr. Hart is also a past-president of the International Association of Director of Law Enforcement Standards and Training.

John D. Boren

John Boren has worked in the Criminal Justice System since 1964 in numerous capacities ranging from large and small city patrol officer to Assistant Police Chief and Bureau Chief of Basic and Advanced Training. He has been an academy instructor for 19 years, teaching basic, advanced and instructor development programs in areas such as firearms, defensive tactics, patrol, ethics, officer survival and the use of force (lethal and non-lethal). Mr. Boren has co-developed the Defensive Tactics program that has been adopted as the State Training Standard by Oklahoma, Wyoming and New Mexico. Mr. Boren has also served as the State Director of the American Society of Law Enforcement Trainers and the Justice Training Association. He has taught at national seminars for both ASLET and JTA, and has served as an expert witness.